INSTANT POT COOKBOOK FOR TWO

Quick, Easy and Delicious Instant Pot Recipes for Two

Table of Contents

INTRODUCTION

Congratulations on getting your personal copy of *Instant Pot Cookbook for Two: Quick, Easy and Delicious Instant Pot Recipes for Two.*

The Instant Pot is an amazing cooking gadget that can make your life a lot easier when it comes to cooking. If you're in a hurry to make breakfast, lunch or dinner, the Instant Pot can be an excellent timesaver tool to add to your kitchen.

Recipes within this book are all crafted for at least 2 servings that you can use for any occasion and share with that special someone, a family member, a roommate or a friend. This book contains recipes that are easy to make, with ingredients that are commonly found in most grocery stores. You will be able to cook tasty meals even if you have a limited budget or culinary skills.

The following chapters will provide you with countless recipes that you can prepare using your Instant Pot. This book features easy to follow steps and strategies on how to use the Instant Pot to come up with a variety of great recipes. It contains recipes that are healthy, quick and easy to follow.

Lastly, this book contains information on how to use the Instant Pot properly, in case this is your first time using this machine, or you would like to know a few tricks to amplify the use of this cooker.

Thanks again for getting a copy of this book. I hope you enjoy it.

INSTANT POT PRESSURE COOKER BASICS

The **Instant Pot** is a multi-function, countertop 11 psi electric cooker. It can be used as a rice cooker, slow cooker, steamer, warmer, and pressure cooker. Newer models like IP-DUO and IP-SMART have: browning, pasteurization, sautéing, and yogurt making functions.

The **Instant Pot** machines come in three sizes: five, six, and eight quarts. Machines with large capacities are best for making homemade steamed bread and yogurt.

These can be used for pasteurizing milk and for making cheeses. These are also suitable for making large meals for parties, or if you want to freeze large volumes of dishes (e.g. broths, soups, stews, etc.) for later consumption.

Each **Instant Pot** comes with a crockpot (stainless steel inner pot/sleeve,) a removable lid with steaming vent, steaming basket, and a removable trivet.

Benefits of using Instant Pot

1. This is the quintessential set-it-and-walk-away all-in cooker. All you need to do is to:
   - Prepare the ingredients beforehand. Place these into the crock-pot.
   - Twist and lock the lid. Seal or unseal steamer valve (depending on function.)
   - Set desired function (e.g. PRESSURE COOK, STEAM, etc.). Set the timer.
   - Walk away and return after the prescribed cooking time. (See **Note**.)
   - Release the pressure. Remove the lid.
   - Stir in remaining ingredients, if any.
   - Ladle dish into serving containers. Garnish as needed. Serve. Eat.

Note: **Instant Pot** has a "KEEP WARM" (warming) function, which automatically activates after the timer goes off. Unless it is specified in the recipe(s) that you need to turn off the machine *immediately after cooking,* there is no need to rush back to the cooker. You can return to the kitchen whenever you want.

Pressure cooking means that you can cook meals 75% to 100% faster than boiling/braising on the stovetop, and baking/roasting in a conventional oven.

This is especially helpful for vegan meals that entail the use of dried beans, legumes, pulses, etc. Instead of pre-soaking these ingredients for hours prior to use, you can pour these directly into the crockpot, add water, and pressure cook these for several minutes. (See for recommendations.)

2. Use **Instant Pot** to make meals in advance. The machine automatically activates the KEEP WARM function after each cooking cycle. This allows you to prepare meals in the morning, so that you can come home to a warm dinner. Or, set up the **Instant Pot** before going to bed so that breakfast is cooked when you wake up.

How to use the Instant Pot

Instant Pot has automatic: BEAN/CHILI, MEAT/STEW, MULTI-GRAIN, PORRIDGE, POULTRY, PRESSURE, RICE, SAUTE, SLOW COOK, SOUP, STEAM, WARM, and YOGURT functions. (See

For this book, we will concentrate on how to use the PRESSURE or pressure cooker function.

The two easiest ways to do so is to:

<u>**Step 1**</u>:
1. Pour all the ingredients into the crockpot.
2. Close lid. Twist it to lock. Beeping sounds will indicate if machine is sealed.

3. Seal valve (steaming vent) on top of the lid by turning the knob towards the SEALING option (the opposite of which is VENT-ING.) By doing so, the machine automatically assumes that you are opting for NATURAL PRESSURE RELEASE. This means that the lid remains sealed until the pressure within the crockpot dissipates or lessens, extending the cooking time by up to 20 minutes.
4. Press the PRESSURE (pressure cooker) button.
5. Wait for 10 seconds without doing anything. The machine will automatically go to its preset option, which is at: HIGH PRES-SURE at 30 minutes.
6. After the cooking cycle, and the NATURAL PRESSURE RE-LEASE, the machine will automatically activate the KEEP WARM function.
7. This is the only time you can safely open the lid.

Step 2:
1. Pour all the ingredients into the crockpot.
2. Close lid. Twist it to lock. Seal valve.
3. Set machine on MANUAL mode. This still means that you are still pressure cooking, but you can change settings.
4. Choose either LOW PRESSURE or HIGH PRESSURE button. Most of the time though, dishes need to be cooked on high pres-sure.
5. Set the timer by pushing the plus [+] or minus [-] buttons right above the PRESSURE button, to increase or decrease cooking time, respectively.
6. Wait for 10 seconds without doing anything. The machine will then start cooking according to your "instructions."

7. If the recipe calls for turning off the machine immediately after cooking, press the KEEP WARM button twice to CANCEL after the cooking cycle. Or, you can simply unplug the machine.

8. If the recipe recommends QUICK PRESSURE RELEASE, carefully turn the knob on the lid towards VENTING. Keep your face and hands away from the steam as it comes out to prevent second-degree burns. Depending on how much moisture is inside the crockpot, venting can take between fifteen seconds to five minutes.

9. Only when the steam has subsided can you safely open the lid.

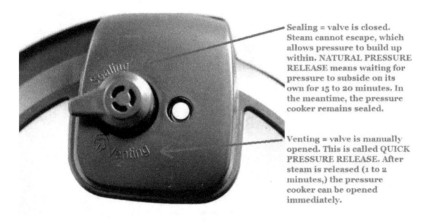

Sealing = valve is closed. Steam cannot escape, which allows pressure to build up within. NATURAL PRESSURE RELEASE means waiting for pressure to subside on its own for 15 to 20 minutes. In the meantime, the pressure cooker remains sealed.

Venting = valve is manually opened. This is called QUICK PRESSURE RELEASE. After steam is released (1 to 2 minutes,) the pressure cooker can be opened immediately.

There are some recipes that require additional steps (e.g. browning, liquid reduction, etc.), so it is best to follow the recommended procedure when cooking.

Important: Instant Pot should have at least one cup of liquid during cooking to prevent contents from sticking to the bottom of the crockpot.

If recipes for pressure cooking require large volumes of liquid, pour in just enough to fill 2/3 of the crockpot. This is to ensure that there is space for pressure and steam to build up within.

For other cooking functions, never fill the pot over the MAX line indicator to avoid spillage.

If you made a mistake with the settings, or you simply want to add a few more ingredients to the crockpot, double press the KEEP WARM button to CANCEL. Opt for a QUICK PRESSURE RELEASE and wait for the steam to subside, if any. Reset the machine as needed.

For other functions and more details: check product manual.

BREAKFAST

01 Poached Eggs and Hash

Prep Time: 8 mins; **Cook Time**: 10 mins
Recommended Serving Size: 1 egg + ½ cup hash; **Serves**: 2

Ingredients:

- 1 c potatoes, cubed
- 1 tsp taco seasoning
- 2 eggs
- 1 tbsp cilantro, chopped
- 1 tbsp bacon, cooked and chopped
- ½ c onion diced
- 2 tbsp butter
- 1 jalapeno, sliced

Directions:

8. Add a cup of water to your pot, and then set the trivet inside.
9. Place your cubed potatoes in a heat safe bowl and set this on top of the trivet.
10. Put the lid on the pot and seal.
11. Set the Instant Pot to high and the timer for two minutes.
12. In the meantime, chop the onion, jalapeno, bacon and cilantro (reserving a little cilantro for finishing).
13. Once the potatoes are done, use the quick pressure release.

14. Remove the bowl of potatoes from the pot, carefully.
15. Remove the water and the trivet carefully and dry out the pot.
16. Set the Instant Pot to sauté and allow it to heat up. Place the butter and onions in the pot and let them cook until the onion becomes translucent.
17. Mix in the pepper, bacon, potatoes, taco seasoning and cilantro.
18. Make two holes in this potato hash mixture and crack an egg into each hole.
19. Lock and seal the lid into place.
20. Set your Instant Pot to high pressure and cook for 1 minute. Once this time is up, use quick release for the pressure.
21. Remove the lid. The eggs will have the consistency of a poached egg. Take the hash out and split the eggs with hash onto two plates, topping the dishes with a sprinkling of cilantro to finish.
22. Serve immediately and enjoy.

02 Egg and Broccoli Casserole

Prep Time: 3 mins; **Cook Time**: 4 hrs
Recommended Serving Size: ¾ cup; **Serves**: 2

Ingredients:

- ¼ tsp salt
- 1½ tbsp onion, finely chopped
- ⅛ c butter, melted
- 2 tbsp all-purpose flour
- 3 eggs, beaten
- 1 c cheddar cheese, shredded (extra to serve)
- 1½ c chopped frozen broccoli, drained and thawed
- 1½ c cottage cheese

Directions:

1. Place all of the above ingredients into a bowl and mix them to-gether. Grease the inside of your pot and pour the mixture into it.
2. Seal the lid and set the Instant Pot to slow cook for one hour on high.
3. At the end of this time, open the pot and stir the mixture.
4. Now close and set the Instant Pot to slow cook on low and leave the casserole to cook for another 3 hours. Sprinkle the top with some extra cheese if you want when serving.

03 Pear Oatmeal

Prep Time: 5 mins; **Cook Time**: 6 mins
Recommended Serving Size: ½ cup; **Serves**: 2

Ingredients:

- ¼ tsp salt
- 1 c milk
- ¼ c walnuts, chopped
- 1 ½ tsp butter, melted
- ¼ c raisins
- 1 c diced pear
- ¼ tsp cinnamon
- ½ c rolled oats
- 2 tbsp brown sugar

Directions:

1. Using a bowl that is heat safe, place all of the ingredients inside the bowl and mix them together.
2. Place a cup of water in your pot and set the trivet inside.
3. Set the bowl on the trivet.
4. Put on the lid and seal in place.
5. Set the Instant Pot to high pressure and cook for 6 minutes.
6. Once the time is up, quick release all of the pressure and carefully remove the bowl.
7. Stir everything together, serve and enjoy.

04 Bread Pudding

Prep Time: 10 mins; **Cook Time**: 25 mins
Recommended Serving Size: 1 cup; **Serves**: 2

Ingredients:

- ½ c sugar
- 6 slices raisin bread, cut into cubes and dried
- cinnamon
- 1 tsp vanilla essence
- 3 eggs
- ½ tsp salt

Directions:

1. Mix together the eggs, cinnamon, salt, sugar and vanilla.
2. Take a five-cup heatproof bowl and grease with butter.
3. Pour the bread cubes into the bowl.
4. Pour the custard mix over the bread and allow this to sit for 15 minutes.
5. Dot the top of the pudding with butter and then cover with aluminum foil.
6. Pour two cups of water into your pot and place in the trivet.
7. Place a foil sling around the bowl and ease the bowl into the pot.
8. Put on the lid and lock into place.
9. Set the Instant Pot to cook at high pressure for 25 minutes.
10. Once this time is up, let the pressure release naturally for 10 minutes and then quick release the rest of the pressure.
11. Carefully take the bowl out.
12. Serve hot.

05 Apple Cranberry Oats

Prep Time: 8 hrs; **Cook Time**: 40 mins
Recommended Serving Size: 1 cup; **Serves**: 2

Ingredients:

- ¼ tsp salt
- 1 c oats
- 1 tsp vanilla essence
- 1 c milk
- ½ c yogurt
- 3 tbsp syrup
- 1 ½ c water
- ¼ tsp nutmeg
- 2 apples, diced
- 1 tsp cinnamon
- ¾ c cranberries
- ½ tsp lemon juice
- 1 tbsp butter

Directions:

1. Grease the instant pot with some butter.
2. Place all of the ingredients into your instant pot, except for the syrup, salt and vanilla essence. Allow the mixture to sit overnight.
3. The following morning, mix in the syrup and salt.
4. Set the Instant Pot to porridge and cook for about 40 minutes.
5. When the time is up, quick-release the pressure.
6. Once the pressure is released, stir in the vanilla and serve.

06 Cinnamon Oatmeal

Prep Time: 5 mins; **Cook Time**: 4 hrs
Recommended Serving Size: 1 cup; **Serves**: 2

Ingredients:

- ¾ c cashews, roasted and chopped
- ½ pint blueberries
- ½ tsp salt
- ¼ tsp nutmeg
- ½ tsp cinnamon
- 1 tsp vanilla essence
- ½ c light brown sugar
- 1 tbsp butter
- 4 c milk
- 1 c steel-cut oats

Directions:

1. Add the salt, nutmeg, cinnamon, vanilla essence, brown sugar, butter, milk and oats to your pot and mix them all together.
2. Put the lid and seal it.
3. Set the Instant Pot to slow cook for 4 hours on low. Once you are ready to serve, mix in the cashews and the blueberries.

07 Orange Steel Cut Oats

Prep Time: 3 mins; **Cook Time**: 16 mins
Recommended Serving Size: ½ cup; **Serves**: 2

Ingredients:

- ¼ c dried cranberries
- ¼ tsp vanilla essence
- ½ c steel cut oats
- 1 tbsp orange zest
- 1 c water
- ¼ tsp cinnamon
- ¼ c orange juice
- 1 tbsp butter
- 1 ½ tsp maple syrup
- 1 c whole milk

Directions:

1. Take a heat safe bowl and mix in all of the above ingredients.
2. Pour a cup of water into your pot and set the trivet inside.
3. Place the bowl on top of the trivet.
4. Put the lid on and lock into place.
5. Set the Instant Pot to high and cook for 6 minutes.
6. Once the time is up, allow the pressure to release naturally for 10 minutes and then use quick release for the remaining pressure.
7. Mix in the cranberries before serving.

08 Egg Muffin

Prep Time: 5 mins; **Cook Time**: 8 mins
Recommended Serving Size: 1 egg each; **Serves**: 2

Ingredients:

- 2 eggs
- 2 crumbled bacon slices
- ¼ tsp lemon pepper seasoning
- Diced onion
- Shredded cheese

Directions:

1. Place 1 ½ cups of water into the bottom of your pot and set in the steamer basket.
2. In two silicon molds, separate the cheese, onion, and bacon.
3. Beat one of the eggs and pour it into one of the molds. Repeat with the other egg.
4. Place the molds in your basket.
5. Put the lid on and seal.
6. Set the Instant Pot to high pressure and cook for 8 minutes.
7. Let the pressure release naturally for 2 minutes and then quick release the rest of the pressure.
8. Enjoy

09 Banana French Toast

Prep Time: 15 mins; **Cook Time**: 25 mins
Recommended Serving Size: 1 cup; **Serves**: 2

Ingredients:

- Maple syrup (to serve)
- ⅛ c pecans, chopped
- 1 tbsp chilled butter, sliced
- ¼ tsp cinnamon
- ½ tsp vanilla essence
- ½ tbsp white sugar
- ¼ c milk
- 2 eggs
- ⅛ c cream cheese
- 1 tbsp brown sugar
- 2 bananas, sliced
- 3 slices French bread, cubed

Directions:

1. Grease a soufflé dish that will fit inside your pot.
2. Place a layer of bread cubes in the bottom of the soufflé dish.
3. Top this layer with half of the banana slices and then sprinkle with half of the brown sugar.
4. Melt the cream cheese in a microwave so that it is spreadable.
5. Spread the cream cheese over the banana and bread layers.
6. Next place the rest of the bread in the bowl and then top this with remaining banana slices.

7. Spread the remainder of the brown sugar over this and then sprinkle with chopped pecans.
8. Lay butter slices over the top of the dish so far.
9. Beat together the eggs and then mix in the cinnamon, vanilla, sugar, and milk.
10. Pour this custard mixture over the butter, making sure that everything is well coated.
11. Place three-quarters of a cup of water into your pot and set in the trivet.
12. Lower the soufflé dish onto the trivet.
13. Put on the lid and lock it into place.
14. Set the Instant Pot to high pressure and let it cook for 25 minutes.
15. Once the time is up, quick release the pressure and then remove the lid.
16. Allow the dish to sit for five to six minutes.
17. Top with extra banana, nuts and maple syrup for serving.

10 Breakfast Hash

Prep Time: 5 mins; **Cook Time**: 15 mins
Recommended Serving Size: 1 cup; **Serves**: 2

Ingredients:

- ½ tsp pepper
- 1 medium potato, diced
- 1 cup bell pepper, chopped
- 1 tsp paprika
- 1 tbsp oil
- 1 medium sweet potato, diced
- pinch of cayenne
- ¼ cup water
- 1 clove minced garlic
- ½ tsp salt
- 1 tsp cumin

Directions:

1. Toss all the potatoes and bell pepper in the spices and oil
2. Put them into the bottom of the pot with a half cup of water.
3. Close and seal the lid.
4. Set the Instant Pot on high and cook for 10 minutes.
5. When finished, quick release the pressure.
6. Reset the Instant Pot to sauté and let the hash mix brown up slightly before serving.

11 Apple Cherry Risotto

Prep Time: 5 mins; **Cook Time**: 20 mins
Recommended Serving Size: 1 cup; **Serves**: 2

Ingredients:

- ½ cup apple juice
- ¾ tsp cinnamon
- ¾ cup Arborio (risotto) rice
- ¼ cup brown sugar
- ¼ cup dried cherries
- 1 tbsp butter
- 1 large apple, peeled, cored, and diced
- 1 ½ cups milk

Directions:

1. Set the Instant Pot to sauté. Add butter to the pot and allow it to melt. This will take about 2-3 minutes.
2. Add in the rice. Continuously stir until the rice turns opaque. This will take about 4 minutes.
3. Then add the apples, spices, and brown sugar, stirring well to combine all the ingredients.
4. Pour in the milk and juice and stir one more time.
5. Close and seal lid.
6. Set the Instant Pot to high pressure and cook for 6 minutes.
7. When the time is up, quick release the pressure. Open and add in the dried cherries and stir well.
8. Spoon into bowls and serve with a splash of milk, sliced almonds and a sprinkle of brown sugar.

MAIN COURSE

12 Chicken Cacciatore

Prep Time: 5 mins; **Cook Time**: 15 mins
Recommended Serving Size: 1 cup; **Serves**: 2

Ingredients:

- ½ c chicken stock
- ¼ c black olives, halved
- ½ tsp salt
- 16-oz can stewed tomatoes
- 1 bay leaf
- ½ tsp oregano
- 3-6 bone-in drumsticks
- ½ tsp garlic (fresh or powder)
- ½ onion, chopped

Directions:

1. Set the Instant Pot to sauté.
2. Place inside the stock, bay leaf and salt. Stir these together and let it warm-up.
3. Place into the pot the following ingredients in this order chicken drumsticks, onion, olives, garlic, oregano and stewed tomatoes. You do not have to stir these together.

4. Put the lid on and lock it into place. Set your Instant Pot on high and cook for 15 minutes.
5. When this time is up, quick release the pressure the stir everything together. The meat will likely fall off the bone.
6. Serve with rice, potato or pasta.

13 Citrus Herb Chicken

Prep Time: 5 mins; **Cook Time**: 15 mins
Recommended Serving Size: ½ chicken portion; **Serves**: 2

Ingredients:

- pinch of pepper
- 2 tbsp white wine
- pinch of salt
- 2 tbsp lemon juice
- pinch of thyme (fresh or dried)
- 1 ¼ lb chicken (whole)
- ¼ c tangerine juice
- ½ tsp rosemary, chopped
- 1 tsp garlic, minced

Directions:

1. Place the chicken into your pot.
2. In a bowl mix together the juices, pepper, wine, salt, garlic, thyme and rosemary. Pour this mixture all over your chicken.
3. Put on the lid and lock it into place.
4. Set the Instant Pot to poultry and cook for 15 minutes.
5. Once this time is up, allow the pressure to release naturally, serve and enjoy.

14 Turkey and Gravy

Prep Time: 10 mins; **Cook Time**: 40 mins
Recommended Serving Size: ½ turkey breast + ½ cup gravy; **Serves**: 2

Ingredients:

- 1 lb turkey breast
- 2 tbsp dry white wine
- 1 ½ tsp tapioca starch
- pinch of salt
- 1 bay leaf
- 1 tbsp butter
- pinch of pepper
- ¾ c chicken broth
- 1 small onion, diced
- 1 tsp dried sage
- 1 carrot, diced
- 1 garlic clove, smashed
- 1 celery stalk, diced

Directions:

1. Rub the turkey breast down with some salt and pepper.
2. Set your Instant Pot to sauté and add in the butter, letting it melt.
3. Lay the turkey breast skin side down in the pot and let it brown. Remove the browned turkey and set to the side.
4. Place the carrot, celery, and onion in your pot. Allow them to cook, stirring often until they soften.
5. Stir in the garlic and sage and let them become fragrant.

6. Mix in the wine and then let the mixture cook for around 3 minutes.
7. Add the bay leaf and broth and deglaze the bottom of the pot.
8. Nestle the turkey breast into the mixture with the skin side up.
9. Put the lid on and lock it into place. Set the Instant Pot to high and cook for 35 minutes. Once this time is up, use the quick pressure release.
10. Remove the turkey breast and tent with foil.
11. Using an immersion blender, add the tapioca starch, stirring the mixture up until smooth.
12. Reset the Instant Pot on sauté and let the gravy cook until it has thickened slightly. For a thicker mixture, stir the tapioca starch with equal parts water together and whisk it into the gravy.
13. Serve the turkey with the gravy.

15 Cranberry Pot Roast

Prep Time: 10 mins; **Cook Time**: 1 hr 20 mins
Recommended Serving Size: 8 oz portion; **Serves**: 2

Ingredients:

- pinch of pepper
- 1 c chicken broth
- 3 whole cloves
- pinch of salt
- 1 cinnamon stick
- 1 lb beef roasting joint
- ½ tsp horseradish powder
- 1 tbsp olive oil
- ¼ c white wine
- 2 tbsp honey
- ½ c cranberries
- ¼ c water

Directions:

1. Rub the beef roast down with salt and pepper.
2. Set your Instant Pot to sauté and pour in the oil, allowing it to heat up.
3. Add in the roast and turn until it is browned all over, then set aside.
4. Pour in the wine and deglaze your pot, making sure that you scrape up all the bits.

5. Mix in the cranberries, cloves, water, garlic, honey, cinnamon and horseradish. Allow this to cook until the cranberries start to burst.
6. Nestle the beef back into the pot and pour in the broth to cover the meat.
7. Put the lid on and lock it in place.
8. Set the Instant Pot to high and cook for 75 minutes.
9. When the time is up, let the pressure release naturally.
10. Serve the pot roast with the cranberry sauce.

16 Lamb with Figs and Ginger

Prep Time: 10 mins; **Cook Time**: 1 hr 20 mins
Recommended Serving Size: 1 lamb shank; **Serves**: 2

Ingredients:

- 1 tbsp coconut oil
- 5 dried figs
- 1 tbsp coconut aminos
- 1 tsp Thai fish sauce (nam pla)
- 2 12-oz lamb shanks
- 1 tbsp apple cider vinegar
- ¾ c chicken broth
- 1 tbsp root ginger, minced
- 1 garlic clove, minced
- 1 medium onion, sliced

Directions:

1. Set your Instant Pot to sauté and pour in the coconut oil.
2. Add in the lamb shanks and turn until they are browned all over, then set aside.
3. Mix the onion and ginger into the pot, allowing them to cook until they soften.
4. Stir in the coconut aminos, garlic, vinegar and fish sauce, deglazing the pot as you go.
5. Then add in the broth and the figs.
6. Set the lamb shanks back into your pot, amongst the liquid.
7. Put on the lid and seal into place.
8. Set the Instant Pot to high and cook for an hour. Once the time is up, allow the pressure to release naturally.

9. Take the shanks out and skim any fat off the top of the liquid. Serve the lamb with the juice.

17 Sous Vide Duck

Prep Time: 2 hrs; **Cook Time**: 23 mins
Recommended Serving Size: 1 duck breast; **Serves**: 2

Ingredients:

- ½ tsp pepper
- ½ tsp peppercorn
- 2 boneless duck breasts
- ½ tsp salt
- 1 tbsp vegetable oil
- 2 tsp garlic, minced
- ½ tsp thyme

Directions:

1. Mix the garlic and spices together and rub over the duck breasts.
2. Place the seasoned duck in the fridge and let it chill for two hours.
3. During the last 20 minutes of the chilling time; fill your Instant Pot up to the seven-cup mark with water and switch the device to keep warm. Allow this to heat for 20 minutes.
4. Rinse all of the spices off the duck breasts.
5. Take a Ziploc bag and place the ducks inside the bag; making sure to remove all the air when you seal it.
6. Place the bag of duck in your Instant Pot in the warm water and let it sit for 38 minutes. You do not have to seal the lid or cook it under pressure. The warm water cooks the duck.
7. Once the time is up, remove the bag and take the duck breasts out. Pat any excess water off the meat.

8. Heat up a large skillet with oil and sear the skin side of the duck. Once the skin side is seared, flip it over and cook on the other side for 20 seconds.
9. Serve and enjoy

18 Barbacoa

Prep Time: 1 hr; **Cook Time**: 45 mins
Recommended Serving Size: 1 cup; **Serves**: 2

Ingredients:

- pinch of salt
- 1 garlic clove, minced
- 1 lb lamb shoulder
- 1 tbsp oil
- 8 oz can enchilada sauce
- 1 small onion, chopped

Directions:

1. Place the lamb in a bag and cover with the enchilada sauce, and allow it to marinate for at least an hour.
2. Set your Instant Pot to sauté and heat up the oil.
3. Lay the onions into your pot and cook until they becomes soft.
4. Mix the garlic in and allow it to become fragrant.
5. Place the lamb along with the enchilada sauce into the pot and allow the mixture to come to the boil.
6. Put the lid on and lock it into place.
7. Reset the Instant Pot to stew and cook for 36 minutes.
8. When the time is up, quick-release the pressure.
9. Remove the lamb and shred. Mix the shredded lamb back into the sauce and serve with rice.

19 Indian Kadhi

Prep Time: 10 mins; **Cook Time**: 4 hrs 10 mins
Recommended Serving Size: 1 ½ cups; **Serves**: 2

Ingredients:

- ¼ c gramflour
- ½ tsp turmeric
- ½ c yogurt
- ½ tsp salt
- 3 c water

Seasoning:

- ¼ tsp fenugreek seeds
- 2 dry red chilies
- ½ tsp ajwain seeds

Directions:

1. Place the gram flour, turmeric, yogurt, salt, and water in a blender and mix until they are smooth.
2. Set your Instant Pot to sauté and add in a teaspoon of butter.
3. Once the butter has melted, place in the seasoning ingredients, stirring often until they become aromatic.
4. Mix in the yogurt mixture, making sure it is well combined.
5. Close the lid and place the instant pot to the slow cook setting and set for four hours.
6. Once this is cooked, serve with crunchy boondi.

20 Mongolian Beef

Prep Time: 10 mins; **Cook Time**: 24 mins
Recommended Serving Size: 8 oz portion; **Serves**: 2

Ingredients:

- 1 lb beef flank steak, thinly sliced
- 2 garlic cloves, minced
- 1 tbsp water
- 1 ½ tsp oil
- 1 green onion, chopped
- ¼ tsp ginger, minced
- 1 ½ tsp cornstarch
- ¼ c water
- 1/3 c brown sugar
- ¼ c soy sauce

Directions:

1. Sprinkle the strips of meat with salt and pepper.
2. Set your Instant Pot to sauté and add in the oil.
3. Once the oil is hot, start browning the meat in batches. Set the browned meat to the side.
4. Place the garlic in the pot and let it cook for a minute.
5. Mix in the soy sauce, ½ cup water, ginger and brown sugar, making sure everything is very well combined.
6. Add the beef back in.
7. Close the lid and seal it into place.
8. Set the Instant Pot to high pressure and cook for 12 minutes.
9. When the time is up, use quick pressure release.

10. Mix together the remaining water and the cornstarch and stir this into the pot. Allow it to cook until it has thickened slightly.
11. Stir in the green onions before serving.

21 Braised Turkey

Prep Time: 5 mins; **Cook Time**: 1 hour 15 mins
Recommended Serving Size: 1 turkey thigh; **Serves**: 2

Ingredients:

- 2 turkey thighs
- ¼ tsp each rosemary, pepper, sage, salt and thyme
- ½ c chicken broth
- 1 tsp garlic, minced
- ½ c onion slices
- 1 ½ tsp red wine vinegar
- ½ c portobello mushrooms

Gravy:

- 3 tbsp flour
- ¼ c water

Directions:

1. Set your Instant Pot to sauté.
2. Once it is heated, add in the turkey and brown.
3. Then add in all of the remaining ingredients, except for the water and flour.
4. Close the lid and lock it into place.
5. Set the Instant Pot to poultry and cook for 1 hour.
6. When the time is up, quick-release the pressure and check to see if your turkey is done.
7. If it doesn't reach the correct internal temperature, then cook it for another 15 minutes.

8. Once the turkey is cooked through, take it out and tent with aluminum foil.

9. Whisk together the flour and water and mix this into the liquid in the pot.

10. Set the Instant Pot to warm and allow the gravy to simmer for about 15 minutes.

11. Slice the turkey and serve covered with the gravy.

22 Polynesian Chicken

Prep Time: 10 mins; **Cook Time**: 12 mins
Recommended Serving Size: 1 sandwich; **Serves**: 2

Ingredients:

- 2 boneless chicken breasts
- 1 medium pineapple, sliced, set 2 slices aside and chop the rest into chunks.
- 3 oz orange juice concentrate
- 2 hamburger buns
- 1 ½ lemons, juiced
- ¾ tsp cornstarch
- ¼ tsp soy sauce
- 1 tbsp brown sugar
- 3 oz peaches

Directions:

1. Stir together the peaches, orange juice, brown sugar, soy sauce, pineapple chunks and lemon juice.
2. Add half of this into your Instant Pot.
3. Lay your chicken inside the pot.
4. Cover the chicken with the remainder of the mixture.
5. Put the lid on and lock it into place.
6. Set the Instant Pot to high pressure and allow it to cook for 12 minutes.
7. When the time is up, quick-release the pressure.
8. Remove the chicken breasts and shred.
9. Remove the fruit pieces from the juices.

10. Take a tablespoon of the juice and mix in the cornstarch. Add this mix back into the remaining juice in the pot.
11. Reset the Instant Pot to sauté and cook the sauce until it has thickened. Mix in the shredded chicken to coat.
12. Split the chicken between the hamburger buns and top with a grilled pineapple.

23 Provincial Chicken

Prep Time: 5 mins; **Cook Time**: 8 hours, 15 minutes
Recommended Serving Size: 1 cup; **Serves**: 2

Ingredients:

- 2 boneless skinless chicken breasts
- 2 cups dried pasta, (bow tie or spiral shapes)
- 1 can diced tomatoes
- ¼ cup sour cream
- 1 zucchini, diced
- ½ tsp basil
- 1 can cream of chicken soup
- 1 tbsp parsley
- ½ cup cheddar cheese, grated
- ½ tbsp minced dried onion
- 1 tbsp balsamic vinegar

Directions:

1. Place the pasta, herbs, chicken, onion, tomatoes, vinegar, zucchini and soup in the bottom of the Instant Pot.
2. Close and seal the lid.
3. Set the Instant Pot on slow cook for 8 hours on low.
4. When the time is up, quick release the pressure.
5. Remove the chicken and shred with two forks.
6. Add the chicken back into the pot with the cheese and sour cream. Stir to combine everything.
7. Reset the Instant Pot to sauté. Let this cook another 15 minutes until heated through and the cheese has melted.
8. Serve and enjoy.

24 Salt Baked Chicken

Prep Time: 5 mins; **Cook Time**: 20 mins
Recommended Serving Size: 2 chicken legs; **Serves**: 2

Ingredients:

- 4 chicken legs
- pinch of pepper
- 1 tsp dried ground ginger
- ⅛ tsp five spice powder
- ½ tsp kosher salt

Directions:

1. Rub chicken with five spice powder, ginger, salt and pepper. Wrap each chicken leg individually with parchment paper and place in a shallow heat proof dish.
2. Add 1 cup of water to the bottom of the Instant Pot and place in the trivet.
3. Sit the dish of chicken on the steamer rack.
4. Close and seal the lid.
5. Set the Instant Pot on high pressure for 20 minutes.
6. When the time is up, quick release the pressure.
7. Remove the chicken dish carefully, unwrap and serve.

SOUPS AND STEWS

25 Jalapeno Chicken Chili

Prep Time: 8 mins; **Cook Time**: 13 mins
Recommended Serving Size: 1 cup; **Serves**: 2

Ingredients:

- ¼ c corn chips
- ½ c jalapeno, diced
- 2 tbsp pepper jack cheese
- 1 ½ tsp garlic, minced
- ¾ c onion, diced
- ½ tsp oregano
- 1 ¾ c cooked chicken
- ½ c cooked bacon, chopped
- ½ tsp cumin
- 1 tsp chili powder
- 7 oz corn
- 1 can tomatoes, chopped
- 4 oz cream cheese
- pinch of salt
- 1 c chicken broth
- pinch of pepper

Directions:

1. Place the onion, corn, jalapeno, tomatoes, garlic, broth, cooked chicken, oregano, chili powder, pepper, cumin and salt in the pot and mix it together.
2. Put on the lid and lock into place.
3. Set your Instant Pot to soup for 10 minutes.
4. Once the time is up, quick-release the pressure.
5. Reset the Instant Pot to warm and stir in the cream cheese and half of the chopped bacon. Let the mixture cook for about 3 minutes.
6. Serve with a topping of chips, cheese and the remaining bacon.

26 Chicken Taco Soup

Prep Time: 10 mins; **Cook Time**: 20 mins
Recommended Serving Size: 1 cup; **Serves**: 2

Ingredients:

- 8 oz black beans, rinsed
- 4 oz tomato sauce
- 2 c chicken, diced
- 8 oz chili beans
- ¾ oz taco seasoning
- 10 oz tomatoes with green chilies, drained
- ½ c onion, diced

Directions:

1. Place all of the above ingredients into your Instant Pot and stir everything together.
2. Put the lid on and lock into place.
3. Set the Instant Pot to soup and cook for 10 minutes.
4. Let the pressure release naturally for 10 minutes, and then quick release the rest of the pressure.
5. Stir everything again, serve and enjoy.

27 Chicken Stew

Prep Time: 8 mins; **Cook Time**: 20 mins
Recommended Serving Size: 1 ½ cup; **Serves**: 2

Ingredients:

- ½ c kale, chopped
- ¼ c onion, diced
- 8 oz tomatoes, diced
- ½ c leek, diced
- 1 tbsp olive oil
- pinch of oregano
- 2 tsp garlic, minced
- pinch of basil
- ½ c carrot, diced
- ¼ tsp red pepper flakes
- 2 c chicken broth
- ¼ tsp paprika
- ½ c red potato, chopped
- ½ tsp thyme
- ½ c celery, diced
- 8 oz garbanzo beans
- 1 ½ c chicken, shredded

Directions:

1. Set the Instant Pot to sauté. Place in the onions, garlic and leeks and allow them to sauté for a while until they become translucent.
2. Stir in the celery and carrots, and cook until softened.

3. Mix in the stock, kale, potatoes, tomatoes, chicken, oregano, garbanzo beans, basil, thyme, pepper flakes and paprika.
4. Put on the lid and seal into place.
5. Set your Instant Pot to soup and cook for 10 minutes.
6. When the time is up, quick release the pressure and stir everything together before serving.

28 Beef Stew

Prep Time: 15 mins; **Cook Time**: 50 mins
Recommended Serving Size: 1 cup; **Serves**: 2

Ingredients:

- ¾ lb chuck roast, diced
- ¼ tsp garlic powder
- ½ tbsp oil
- ½ onion, chunked
- ¼ tsp salt
- ¼ lb baby carrots
- 4 oz tomato sauce
- ¼ lb potatoes, chunked
- ¼ tsp smoked paprika
- 4 oz chicken stock

Directions:

1. Set the Instant Pot to sauté, add in the oil and let it warm.
2. Place the meat in the pot and brown it up. As it is browning, add in the salt.
3. Once the meat has browned, mix in the paprika, stock and tomato sauce.
4. Set your Instant Pot to manual and cook for 15 minutes.
5. When the time is up, quick release the pressure and mix in all of the vegetables.
6. Keep the Instant Pot to manual and cook for another 30 minutes.
7. When this time is up, quick release the pressure, mix everything together and enjoy.

29 Chicken Tortilla Soup

Prep Time: 10 mins; **Cook Time**: 20 mins
Recommended Serving Size: 1 cup; **Serves**: 2

Ingredients:

- 2 c chicken broth
- ½ lb chicken breasts
- 1 tbsp oil
- ⅛ tsp cayenne pepper
- 1 garlic clove, minced
- 15 oz can black beans
- 6-in corn tortilla, chopped (and one to serve, sliced)
- 1 tbsp cilantro, chopped
- ½ c frozen corn
- ½ tsp cumin
- 1 tsp chili powder
- 1 small onion, chopped
- 1 tomato, chopped

Directions:

1. Set your Instant Pot to sauté. Add in the oil and onion, cooking until it becomes soft.
2. Mix in the cilantro, tortilla squares and garlic. Stir and cook for another minute.
3. Add in the spices, beans, chicken, tomato and broth, stirring everything together.
4. Put the lid on and lock into place.
5. Reset the Instant Pot to soup and cook for 4 minutes

6. As the soup is cooking, prep your side items.
7. Take the extra tortilla and slice into strips. Cook the strips in some hot oil. Remove these carefully and place on a paper towel, top with some salt.
8. After the chili is done, quick release the pressure.
9. Remove the chicken and shred it. Stir this back into the mixture.
10. Top the chili soup with tortilla strips, cheese and cilantro to serve.

30 Texas Chili

Prep Time: 15 mins; **Cook Time**: 50 mins
Recommended Serving Size: 1 ½ cups; **Serves**: 2

Ingredients:

- pinch of salt
- 2.5 lbs beef chuck, cubed
- 1 medium onion, diced
- pinch of pepper
- 1 ½ tsp kosher salt
- 14.5 oz can crushed tomatoes
- 1 lime, juiced
- 2 tbsp masa harina
- 2 garlic cloves, minced
- 1 ½ tsp oil
- ½ c coffee
- ¼ tsp kosher salt
- 1 tsp oregano
- ¼ c chili powder
- 1 chipotle en adobo, minced
- 1 tbsp cumin

Directions:

1. Set your Instant Pot to sauté and heat up the oil.
2. Rub the cubes of beef with some salt and brown them in batches in the pot. Make sure the pot isn't overcrowded, and only brown them on one side. Remove with a slotted spoon and set to the side.

3. Put the onions into the pot and season them with a little bit of salt. Allow them to cook until they become soft, making sure you scrape up all of the caramelized bits on the bottom as they cook.
4. Stir in the chipotle and garlic and let it all cook for 1 minute.
5. Slide the mixture to the edges of the pot and add the cumin, oregano and chili powder into your newly made hole.
6. Let this cook until the mixture becomes fragrant, and then mix it into the onion mixture.
7. Add in the coffee and deglaze the pot.
8. Place the meat and all the rest of the ingredients into the pot and stir it all together, making sure the meat is coated well in the sauce.
9. Put the lid on and seal it into place.
10. Set the Instant Pot to high pressure and cook for 30 minutes.
11. When the time is up, let the pressure release naturally.
12. Optional Step: Place the chili in a bowl and allow it to refrigerate overnight. The next morning, scrape the solid fat off the top and then bring to a simmer in a pot before continuing.
13. Take a cup of the liquid out of the chili and mix in the masa harina and lime juice.
14. Mix this back into the pot and add salt to taste.
15. Serve and enjoy.

31 Tomato Soup

Prep Time: 5 mins; **Cook Time**: 5 mins
Recommended Serving Size: 1 cup; **Serves**: 2

Ingredients:

- 14 oz crushed tomatoes
- pinch of salt
- 14 oz whole tomatoes
- pinch of pepper
- 1 ½ c water
- 1 ½ tsp agave
- ¼ c cashew pieces
- 2 garlic cloves, minced
- 1 ½ tbsp oats
- 1 ½ tsp basil
- 1 vegetarian bouillon cube

Directions:

1. Place all of the above ingredients into your pot, except for the salt, agave, and pepper.
2. Put on the lid and lock it into place.
3. Set the Instant Pot to high pressure and cook for 5 minutes.
4. When the time is up, quick-release the pressure and remove the lid.
5. Next, take an immersion blender to puree the mixture up to your desired consistency. You can also blend it up with a regular blender if you would prefer to use one.
6. Place everything into a serving dish and mix in the agave, pepper, salt and adjust any flavors that you need to.

32 Chicken Noodle Soup

Prep Time: 10 mins; **Cook Time**: 40 mins
Recommended Serving Size: 1 cup; **Serves**: 2

Ingredients:

- pinch of pepper
- 1 chicken breast
- ½ bag kluski noodles
- ¼ lb carrots, sliced
- 1 celery stalk, sliced
- pinch of salt
- 1 small potato, chopped
- 1 ½ tsp chicken bouillon
- ¼ c onion, chopped
- 3 c water

Directions:

1. Add the chicken, onion, noodles, carrot, potato, and celery to the pot.
2. Pour the water over everything and drop in the bouillon cube.
3. Put on the lid and lock it into place.
4. Set your Instant Pot to soup and cook for 40 minutes.
5. When the time is up, allow the pressure to release naturally for 10 minutes and then quick release the rest of the pressure.
6. Take the chicken out and shred it.
7. Mix the shredded chicken back into the soup.
8. Season with some pepper and salt to taste and enjoy.

33 Beef Stew

Prep Time: 10 mins; **Cook Time**: 55 mins
Recommended Serving Size: 1 cup; **Serves**: 2

Ingredients:

- ¾ lb chuck roast, cubed
- ¼ tsp garlic powder
- ½ tbsp oil
- ½ onion, chunked
- ¼ tsp kosher salt
- ¼ lb baby carrots
- 4 oz tomato sauce
- ¼ lb potatoes, chunked
- ¼ tsp smoked paprika
- 4 oz chicken stock

Directions:

1. Set your Instant Pot to sauté, add in the oil, cooking until it gets hot.
2. Place the roast chunks into the pot and salt the roast while you brown the meat.
3. Once the meat has browned up, add in the paprika, stock and tomato sauce.
4. Put the lid on and lock it into place.
5. Set the Instant Pot to manual and cook for 15 minutes.
6. When the time is up, quick release the pressure.
7. Mix in all of the vegetables.
8. Put the lid back on and lock it into place.

9. Keep the Instant Pot set to manual and cook for 30 more minutes.
10. When this time is up, release the pressure however you would like and enjoy.

34 Curried Chicken Soup

Prep Time: 10 mins; **Cook Time**: 25 mins
Recommended Serving Size: 1 cup; **Serves**: 2

Ingredients:

- 2 lime wedges
- 1 c onion, diced
- 1 tbsp olive oil
- 1 c basmati rice
- 1 tbsp peanut butter
- 1 c carrot, sliced
- 2 tbsp cilantro
- 1 ½ c bell pepper, sliced
- 1 tbsp soy sauce
- 1 ½ c cooked chicken, diced
- ¾ c coconut milk
- 1 ½ tsp ginger, minced
- ½ tsp sucanat
- ¾ tbsp lemongrass
- 2 tsp garlic, minced
- 1 tbsp sriracha
- 1 ½ tsp curry powder
- 2 c chicken broth
- ½ tsp salt

Directions:

1. Set your Instant Pot to sauté, add in the oil and allow it to heat up.

2. Add in the carrot, pepper and onion, and cook them until they have softened.
3. Mix in the garlic, curry powder and ginger; cooking until the spices have become fragrant.
4. Mix in the salt, broth and lemongrass and let the mixture come up to the boil.
5. Mix in the chicken cubes, peanut butter, soy sauce, sriracha, sucanant and milk.
6. Put the lid on and lock it into place.
7. Set the Instant Pot to manual for 3 minutes.
8. When the time is up, quick release the pressure.
9. Serve the soup over rice, topped with cilantro and a lime wedge.

35 Carrot and Turnip Stew

Prep Time: 10 mins; **Cook Time**: 15 mins
Recommended Serving Size: 1 cup; **Serves**: 2

Ingredients:

- ½ lb beef stewing steak
- 2 tbsp parsley
- pinch of salt
- 2 tbsp coconut aminos
- 1 tbsp butter
- ½ lb carrots, chopped
- 1 small onion, chopped
- ½ lb turnips, chopped
- 1 tbsp cassava flour
- ½ c chicken broth
- ½ tsp thyme
- ½ c red wine

Directions:

1. Sprinkle the meat with some salt.
2. Set your Instant Pot to sauté and add in half of the butter, allowing it to melt.
3. Add the beef into the pot and brown completely. Then set it aside.
4. Add in the rest of the butter and the onions to the pot and cook until they are soft.
5. Stir in the flour and thyme.
6. Mix in the wine, and deglaze the pot.

7. Stir in the broth, browned beef, turnips, coconut aminos and carrots.
8. Put on the lid and lock into place.
9. Reset the Instant Pot to high pressure and cook for 15 minutes.
10. Once the time is up, quick release the pressure and serve the stew.

36 Borscht Soup

Prep Time: 5 mins; **Cook Time**: 45 mins
Recommended Serving Size: 1 cup; **Serves**: 2

Ingredients:

- 1 tbsp olive oil
- ½ tsp sugar
- 1 medium beet
- squeeze of ketchup
- 1 tsp garlic, minced
- pinch of pepper
- ½ tsp dill
- 1 small onion, chopped
- pinch of salt
- ½ cup broth
- ¼ cup sauerkraut
- ½ tsp red wine vinegar
- 1 red cubed potato

To finish:

parsley
sour cream

Directions:

1. Place the steamer basket into the bottom of the Instant Pot.
2. Pour in one and a half cups water.
3. Put the beet into the steamer basket.
4. Close and seal lid.

5. Set to high pressure and cook for 30 minutes.
6. When the time is up, quick release the pressure.
7. Carefully remove the beet and place in cold water. When the beet is cool enough to handle, put on disposable gloves and peel. Dice the peeled beet.
8. Pour the water out of the pot.
9. Reset the Instant Pot to sauté and add in the oil. When the oil has warmed, then add in dill, salt, pepper, parsley, and onions. Cook until everything is fragrant.
10. Add in the tomatoes, beets, potatoes, carrots, garlic, and sauerkraut. Stir everything well.
11. Pour in the broth and stir again.
12. Add in the ketchup, sugar, and vinegar. Stir one more time.
13. Give it a taste and adjust any seasoning you need to.
14. Close and seal lid.
15. Reset the Instant Pot to high and cook for 10 minutes
16. . When this time is up, quick release the pressure.
17. Spoon the borscht into serving bowls and serve with a sprinkling of parsley and a dollop of sour cream to finish.

37 Taco Soup

Prep Time: 5 mins; **Cook Time**: 10 mins
Recommended Serving Size: 1 cup; **Serves**: 2

Ingredients:

- 1/3 cup onion, diced
- 1 cup black beans
- ¾ cup cooked ground beef
- ½ cup water
- ¼ tsp salt
- 1 cup pinto beans
- ¼ tsp pepper
- 5 oz. diced tomatoes with green chilies
- ¼ oz ranch dressing mix
- 8 oz diced tomatoes
- ½ tbsp taco seasoning
- 4 oz corn

To finish:

shredded cheese
sour cream

Directions:

1. Put all the ingredients into the Instant Pot.
2. Stir well to combine.
3. Close and seal the lid.
4. Set the Instant Pot to soup and cook for 10 minutes.
5. When the time is up, quick release the pressure.
6. Spoon into bowls and top with sour cream and cheese to serve.

ONE POT MEALS

38 Cheeseburger Meatball Sandwiches

Prep Time: 5 mins; **Cook Time**: 6 mins
Recommended Serving Size: 1 sandwich; **Serves**: 2

Ingredients:

- ½ lb ground beef
- ¾ c cheddar cheese (to serve)
- 2 tbsp breadcrumbs
- 2 tbsp onion, minced
- 2 sub rolls
- 1 egg, beaten
- ½ tsp chili powder
- pinch of pepper
- 1 ½ tsp steak seasoning
- pinch of garlic salt
- 8 oz tomato sauce
- ¼ c bell pepper, diced
- 1 ½ tsp mustard
- 1 ½ tsp Worcestershire sauce
- ¼ c onion, diced
- 1 tbsp brown sugar

Directions:

1. Mix together the beef, egg, breadcrumbs, minced onion and steak seasoning. Shape this mixture into meatballs.
2. Place all the other ingredients, minus the rolls and cheese, into your pot.
3. Add the meatballs into the tomato mixture.
4. Put the lid on the pot and lock it into place.
5. Set the Instant Pot to high and cook for 6 minutes.
6. When the time is up, quick release the pressure.
7. Split the meatballs between the rolls and top with cheese to serve.

39 Jambalaya

Prep Time: 8 mins; **Cook Time**: 17 mins
Recommended Serving Size: 1 ½ cup; **Serves**: 2

Ingredients:

- ¼ lb andouille sausage, diced
- ¼ lb chicken, diced
- ¾ tsp Worcestershire sauce
- ¼ lb prawns
- Olive oil
- 1 ¾ tsp Creole seasoning
- ½ c onion, diced
- ¼ c crushed tomatoes
- ½ c bell pepper, diced
- ¾ c chicken stock
- 1 ½ tsp garlic, minced
- 1/3 c rice

Directions:

1. Set your Instant Pot to sauté.
2. As it heats, sprinkle the chicken with a teaspoon of the Creole seasoning.
3. Place the chicken in the pot and brown the chicken up. Set the browned chicken aside.
4. Mix in the pepper, garlic and onions to the pot and allow this to sauté until the onions become translucent.
5. Mix in the rice, and let it cook for another 2 minutes.

6. Add the chicken, tomato puree, remaining Creole seasoning and Worcestershire sauce and mix everything together.
7. Put the lid on and lock it into place.
8. Set the Instant Pot to rice and allow it to cook (about 10 minutes).
9. Once the rice is done, release the pressure and mix in the sausage and prawns.
10. Put the lid back on.
11. Reset the Instant Pot to manual and let this cook for 2 minutes.

40 Tuna Noodle Delight

Prep Time: 8 mins; **Cook Time**: 18 mins
Recommended Serving Size: 1 cup; **Serves**: 2

Ingredients:

- pinch of parsley
- ½ c onion, chopped
- Feta cheese (to serve)
- 8 oz egg noodles
- 1 jar artichoke hearts
- 1 tbsp oil
- 1 c diced tomatoes
- 1 can tuna, drained
- 1 ¼ c water
- 1/8 tsp pepper
- ¼ tsp salt

Directions:

1. Set your Instant Pot to sauté, add in the oil and heat
2. Place in the onion and let it cook for 2 minutes.
3. Mix in the pepper, noodles, tomatoes, salt and water.
4. Reset the Instant Pot to soup and cook for 10 minutes.
5. When this time is up, quick release the pressure.
6. Mix in the tuna and artichokes.
7. Reset the Instant Pot to sauté and let it cook for 4 minutes, or until the tuna and artichokes have warmed through.
8. Serve with parsley and feta cheese.

41 Chicken with Sweet Potato and Squash

Prep Time: 3 mins; **Cook Time**: 9 mins
Recommended Serving Size: 1 ½ cup; **Serves**: 2

Ingredients:

- ¾ c sweet potato, peeled and diced
- pinch of pepper
- ½ lb chicken, cubed
- pinch of salt
- 1 tsp garlic, minced
- 3 c butternut squash, peeled and chunked
- 3 tbsp basil
- ½ c chicken broth
- 3 tbsp parsley

Directions:

1. Place everything from the above list into your pot and mix together.
2. Put the lid on and lock into place.
3. Set the Instant Pot to poultry and cook for 9 minutes.
4. When the time is up , quick release the pressure and serve.

42 Pozole Rojo

Prep Time: 8 mins; **Cook Time**: 6 hrs 10 mins
Recommended Serving Size: 1 cup; **Serves**: 2

Ingredients:

- ½ lb pork, cubed
- 1 lime wedge (to serve)
- 1 tbsp vegetable oil
- pinch of salt
- ½ small onion, diced
- 4 oz can diced green chilies
- pinch of pepper
- 16 oz can hominy
- pinch of oregano
- 8 oz can enchilada sauce
- 1 garlic clove, minced
- ½ tsp cumin
- 1 c chicken broth
- ½ chipotle in adobo

Directions:

1. Sprinkle the salt and pepper over the pork.
2. Set your Instant Pot to sauté and heat up the oil.
3. Place the garlic and onions in the oil and cook until the onions become translucent and the garlic fragrant.
4. Stir in all the other ingredients, minus the lime.
5. Reset the Instant Pot to high and cook for 6 hours.
6. When this time is up, release the pressure and top with some fresh lime juice to serve.

43 Corned Beef and Cabbage

Prep Time: 10 mins; **Cook Time**: 1 hr 40 mins
Recommended Serving Size: 16 oz; **Serves**: 2

Ingredients:

- 2 lb corned beef brisket
- 1 small cabbage head, wedged
- 2 c water
- 1 medium carrot, chunked
- ½ small onion, chopped
- ½ lb potatoes
- 2 garlic cloves, smashed
- ½ tsp thyme
- 1 bay leaf
- ¼ tsp whole allspice
- 2 whole peppercorns

Directions:

1. Place the brisket, thyme, water, allspice, onion, garlic and peppercorns into your Instant Pot.
2. Put the lid on and lock it into place.
3. Set the Instant pot to high pressure and cook for 90 minutes.
4. When the time is up, allow the pressure to release naturally.
5. Take the meat out and set it aside, covered with foil.
6. Place the carrots, cabbage and potatoes into your pot.
7. Put the lid back on and lock into place.
8. Reset the Instant Pot to high pressure and cook for another 10 minutes.

9. When this time is up, quick release the pressure and remove the lid.
10. Take out the vegetables and serve alongside the beef.

44 Indian Curry

Prep Time: 10 mins; **Cook Time**: 50 mins
Recommended Serving Size: 1 cup; **Serves**: 2

Ingredients:

- 2 c goat shoulder
- pinch of salt
- 8 garlic cloves, minced
- 1 ¼ c water
- 2 small onions, chopped
- 3 tbsp curry powder
- pinch of pepper
- 1 medium shallot, chopped
- 1/3 c tomato paste
- 1 tbsp ginger
- 1 tbsp cilantro
- 1 medium potato
- ¼ tsp Indian chili powder
- 2 tbsp olive oil

Directions:

1. Place your Instant Pot to sauté and heat up some olive oil.
2. Add in the goat and sprinkle with salt and pepper, brown up the shoulder.
3. Set the shoulder meat to the side.
4. Mix the onion, shallots and ginger into the pot with a little more olive oil.
5. Mix in the garlic and allow it to cook until it becomes fragrant.

6. Mix in the chili pepper and curry powder, cooking until they become fragrant.
7. Mix in a quarter cup of water and deglaze the pot.
8. Mix all the rest of the water in.
9. Place the tomato paste, goat and potatoes into the pot, but do not stir them together.
10. Put on the lid and lock it into place.
11. Set the Instant Pot to high pressure and cook for 36 minutes.
12. When this time is up, allow the pressure to release completely
13. Break the potato up to help thicken the sauce.
14. Mix in the cilantro, and adjust any seasonings to taste then serve with rice.

45 Sausage and Pasta

Prep Time: 5 mins; **Cook Time**: 15 mins
Recommended Serving Size: 1 cup; **Serves**: 2

Ingredients:

- olive oil
- 2 tbsp parmesan, grated
- ¼ c bacon
- handful of basil
- 1 c sausage meat
- enough water to cover pasta
- ½ onion, chopped
- 1 c dried pasta
- 1 garlic clove, minced
- pinch of salt
- 1 c tomato puree

Directions:

1. Set your Instant Pot to sauté and add in the oil to heat.
2. Place in the bacon and cook until crispy. Once cooked remove the bacon and drain on a paper towel.
3. Add in the sausage and cook until it is browned.
4. Mix in the onion and garlic. While cooking, make sure you scrape the caramelized bits from the bottom of you pot.
5. Cancel the sauté setting and mix in the salt and tomato.
6. Stir in the pasta and make sure it is well coated in the sauce.
7. Add in the water until the pasta is completely covered.
8. Put on the lid and lock it into place.
9. Reset the Instant Pot to low pressure and cook for 5 minutes.

10. When this time is up, quick release the pressure.
11. Stir in the basil and the cheese to serve and enjoy.

46 Cassoulet

Prep Time: 10 mins; **Cook Time**: 40 mins
Recommended Serving Size: 1 cup; **Serves**: 2

Ingredients:

- 2 garlic cloves, minced
- 1 lb pork ribs, chunked
- 1 c great northern beans
- 1 tbsp rosemary
- ½ c beef broth
- 1 tbsp olive oil
- ¼ onion, diced
- 1 c herb croutons (to serve)
- 1 carrot, diced
- ½ celery stalk, diced

Directions:

1. Set your Instant Pot to sauté.
2. Rub the rib meat with salt and pepper, then place in your pot to brown up.
3. Mix in the onion, broth, garlic, celery, rosemary, beans and carrots.
4. Put on the lid and lock into place.
5. Reset the Instant Pot to manual and cook for 35 minutes.
6. When this time is up, quick release the pressure.
7. Serve the cassoulet topped with the croutons.

47 French Dip Sandwiches

Prep Time: 20 mins; **Cook Time**: 35 mins
Recommended Serving Size: 1 sandwich; **Serves**: 2

Ingredients:

- 2 lb roast beef
- 2 hamburger buns
- 1 ½ tsp rosemary
- ½ tsp garlic, minced
- 1/3 c soy sauce
- 1 tsp peppercorns
- ½ tsp beef bouillon

Directions:

1. Trim any excess fat from the roast that you can see, and place it into your pot.
2. Place the garlic, soy sauce, rosemary, bouillon, and peppercorns together in a bowl and mix.
3. Pour this peppercorn mixture over your roast.
4. Add in enough water to completely cover the roast.
5. Put the lid on and seal it into place.
6. Set your Instant Pot to beef and cook for 35 minutes.
7. When the time is up, allow the pressure to release naturally.
8. Take the beef out and shred it.
9. Place the shredded beef in the hamburger buns and enjoy.

48 Minestrone

Prep Time: 5 mins; **Cook Time**: 15 mins
Recommended Serving Size: 1 cup; **Serves**: 2

Ingredients:

- 2 c broth
- ¼ c parmesan, grated (to serve)
- 1 stalk celery, diced
- 1 bay leaf
- ½ c pasta
- 1 small carrot, diced
- ¼ c spinach
- 1 tbsp butter
- 1 garlic clove, minced
- 1 small onion, diced
- 1 c white beans
- ½ tsp basil
- ½ tsp oregano
- 15 oz tomatoes
- pinch of pepper
- pinch of salt

Directions:

1. Set your Instant Pot to sauté and heat the oil.
2. Mix in the onion, garlic, carrot, and celery and allow to cook until softened.
3. Mix in the basil, pepper, oregano, and salt.
4. Stir in the bay leaf, broth, pasta, tomatoes, and spinach.

5. Put the lid on and lock in place.
6. Reset the Instant Pot to high pressure and cook for 6 minutes.
7. When the time is up, allow it to rest for a few minutes and then quick release the pressure.
8. Mix in the white beans and serve topped with parmesan.

49 Chicken Lettuce Wraps

Prep Time: 5 mins; **Cook Time**: 10 mins
Recommended Serving Size: 2 wraps; **Serves**: 2

Ingredients:

- pinch of allspice
- 4 romaine lettuce leaves
- ¼ cup water chestnuts, drained
- ½ lb ground chicken
- 2 tbsp coconut aminos
- 2 tbsp chicken broth
- ¼ tsp ground ginger
- 1 ½ tsp garlic, minced
- 1/3 cup onion, diced
- ¼ cup scallions, chopped
- 1 tbsp balsamic vinegar

Directions:

1. Place all ingredients except the lettuce and scallions into the pot. Give everything a good stir.
2. Put on the lid and seal.
3. Set the Instant Pot to manual and cook for 10 minutes.
4. When the time is up, quick release the pressure.
5. Using a potato masher, break up the chicken. Stir everything together.
6. Divide chicken mixture evenly between the lettuce leaves and top with scallions to serve.

50 Lemon Mustard Chicken

Prep Time: 5 mins; **Cook Time**: 15 mins
Recommended Serving Size: 1 thigh; **Serves**: 2

Ingredients:

- 1 lb red potatoes, quartered
- pinch of salt
- ½ cup chicken broth
- 2 tbsp lemon juice
- 1 tbsp Dijon mustard
- 1 tbsp olive oil
- 1 tbsp Italian seasoning
- pinch of pepper
- 1 lb chicken thighs

Directions:

1. Mix the mustard, broth, and juice together.
2. Set the Instant Pot to sauté. Add in some oil and allow it to heat up.
3. Season the chicken thighs with salt and pepper and then place them in the pot. Brown the chicken on all sides.
4. Pour the broth mixture over the chicken. Add in the Italian seasoning and the potatoes.
5. Put the lid on and seal.
6. Set the Instant Pot to high and cook for 15 minutes.
7. When the time is up, quick release the pressure.
8. Serve and enjoy.

GRAINS

51 Beans and Rice

Prep Time: 8 hrs; **Cook Time**: 40 mins
Recommended Serving Size: 1 cup; **Serves**: 2

Ingredients:

- ¼ lb red kidney beans, rinsed
- 1 tsp kosher salt
- 1 pt water

Seasoning

- 1 small onion, minced
- pinch of salt
- 1 tsp oil
- pinch of pepper
- ¼ lb smoked sausage, sliced
- 1 ¼ c water
- ¼ bell pepper, minced
- ¼ tsp kosher salt
- 1 garlic clove, sliced
- ¼ tsp fresh thyme
- ½ celery stalk, chopped
- ½ c cooked rice

To serve:

- hot sauce
- green onion, minced
- chopped parsley

Directions:

1. The night before, soak your beans in water. Sort through them to get rid of broken beans, dirt, and stones. Once rinsed, put them in a large bowl and stir in some salt and place in water so that they are covered.
2. Set your Instant Pot to sauté and add the oil to heat.
3. Place in ¼ teaspoon of salt, sausage, celery, garlic, thyme, pepper, and onion.
4. Stir often, and allow the sausage to cook until it has browned.
5. Drain the water off the beans and rinse again.
6. Add the beans into the pot and add in the bay leaf, ½ teaspoon salt and the water.
7. Put the lid on and lock into place.
8. Reset the Instant Pot to high pressure and cook for 15 minutes.
9. When this time is up, allow the pressure to release naturally, then carefully remove the lid.
10. Discard the bay leaf.
11. Take a half cup of the mixture and puree until smooth.
12. Mix the pureed beans back into the pot and stir.
13. Reset the Instant Pot to sauté, add in the cooked rice and allow the mixture to cook for 15 minutes.
14. Adjust any seasonings to taste.
15. Top with parsley, green onions and hot sauce to serve.

52 Mexican Rice

Prep Time: 2 mins; **Cook Time**: 13 mins
Recommended Serving Size: 1 cup; **Serves**: 2

Ingredients:

- pinch of salt
- ½ avocado
- pinch of pepper
- ½ c cilantro
- 1 c long-grain rice
- ¼ c green salsa
- 1 ¼ c broth

Directions:

1. Place the rice and the broth in your pot and stir it together.
2. Put the lid on and seal it in place.
3. Set the Instant Pot to high pressure and cook for 3 minutes.
4. When the time is up, allow the pressure to release naturally for ten minutes, then quick release the rest of the pressure.
5. Fluff up the rice and let it cool just slightly.
6. Blend together the avocado, salsa, and cilantro until they are smooth.
7. Stir the avocado mixture into the rice.
8. Add extra salt and pepper to taste.

53 Polenta

Prep Time: 1 min; **Cook Time**: 8 mins
Recommended Serving Size: 1 cup; **Serves**: 2

Ingredients:

- ½ c polenta
- ½ tsp salt
- 2 c milk

Creamy Variation extra:

- 3 tbsp butter
- 3 tbsp milk

Directions:

1. Set the Instant Pot to sauté and pour in the two cups of milk.
2. Allow the milk to come up to a boil.
3. Mix in the polenta with the salt to the milk.
4. Put on the lid and lock into place.
5. Reset the Instant Pot to high pressure and cook for 8 minutes.
6. When this time is up, quick release the pressure and serve.
7. For a creamy variation of polenta:
8. Follow the above steps in making the polenta, and once it is cooked, mix in the extra butter and milk.

54 Basmati Rice

Prep Time: 1 min; **Cook Time**: 6 mins
Recommended Serving Size: 1 cup; **Serves**: 2

Ingredients:

- 1 c Indian basmati rice
- 1 c water

Directions:

1. Pour the rice and the water into your pot.
2. Put on the lid and lock into place
3. Set the Instant Pot to high and cook for 6 minutes.
4. When the time is up, quick release the pressure.
5. Fluff the rice up with a fork and serve.

55 Asparagus Risotto

Prep Time: 5 mins; **Cook Time**: 15 mins
Recommended Serving Size: 1 cup; **Serves**: 2

Ingredients:

- ¼ c parmesan, grated
- 2 tbsp orange juice
- 1 small onion, chopped
- ½ c Arborio (risotto) rice
- 2 garlic cloves, chopped
- ½ lb asparagus, diced
- 1 tbsp olive oil
- 1 tbsp thyme
- 1 1/3 c vegetable stock

Directions:

1. Wash your asparagus and chop into half inch pieces.
2. Set the Instant Pot to sauté and add in the oil to heat.
3. Place in the onion and cook until it becomes translucent.
4. Mix the rice and the garlic in. Allow this to sauté until the garlic becomes fragrant.
5. Pour in the stock and the orange juice and stir well.
6. Put on the lid and lock into place.
7. Set the Instant Pot to high and cook for 7 minutes.
8. When the time is up, quick release the pressure.
9. Take the lid off and slowly stir in the asparagus and thyme.
10. Put the lid back on top, you don't have to seal it, and leave it to sit for 5 minutes to soften the asparagus.
11. Place in a serving bowl and mix it together with the grated parmesan to finish.

56 Fried Rice

Prep Time: 2 mins; **Cook Time**: 6 mins
Recommended Serving Size: 1 cup; **Serves**: 2

Ingredients:

- 1 ½ c water
- 1 tbsp soy sauce
- ½ c ham, diced
- 2 tbsp scallions, sliced
- ½ c matchstick carrots
- 1 ½ c brown rice
- 1 tbsp butter

Directions:

1. Place all of the above ingredients in your pot and mix together well.
2. Put on the lid and lock into place.
3. Set the Instant Pot to high pressure and cook for 6 minutes.
4. When the time is up, quick release the pressure and check to make sure the rice is tender, and all the water is absorbed. If not, cook for a few more minutes.
5. After it is cooked through, fluff with a fork and serve.

57 Portuguese Chicken and Rice

Prep Time: 20 mins; **Cook Time**: 20 mins
Recommended Serving Size: 1 cup; **Serves**: 2

Ingredients:

- 3 chicken quarters
- 1 tbsp soy sauce
- 1 ½ tbsp cornstarch slurry
- 1 medium carrot, chunked
- pinch of salt
- 2 potatoes, quartered
- 1 tsp cumin
- 1 onion, sliced
- pinch of pepper
- ¾ c coconut milk
- 1 tbsp peanut oil
- 1 shallot, sliced
- 1 ½ tsp turmeric
- 1 green bell pepper, sliced
- 1 tbsp soy sauce
- 3 garlic cloves, minced
- 2 bay leaves

Marinade:

- 1 tbsp Shaoxing wine
- 1 tbsp soy sauce
- pinch of pepper
- ½ tsp sugar

Rice:

- 1 c water
- 1 c jasmine rice (Thai)

Directions:

1. Combine all of the marinade ingredients together. Add as much pepper as you would like.
2. Put the chicken in a baggie and cover with the marinade, allow this to sit for 20 minutes.
3. Set your Instant Pot to sauté and heat up the oil.
4. Add in the shallots and onion and cook until they have browned, but not burned.
5. Mix in the pepper, garlic, and salt, allow this mixture to continue to cook until you can smell the garlic.
6. Place in the chicken and then let the skin caramelize.
7. Sprinkle in the cumin and the turmeric, and mix everything together until it becomes aromatic.
8. Mix in the potatoes, bay leaves, and carrots.
9. Pour the soy sauce and the milk in, then deglaze the bottom of the pot.
10. Set the steamer rack over top of the chicken.
11. Place the rice and water in a heat safe bowl and mix together.
12. Place the bowl of rice on top of the steamer rack.
13. Put on the lid and lock into place.
14. Set the Instant Pot to high pressure and cook for 4 minutes.
15. Turn off the pot and allow the pressure to release naturally.
16. Once it is done, carefully take out the bowl of rice and fluff. Add as much pepper and salt as your taste buds like.
17. Take the chicken out of the sauce and mix in some extra pepper.
18. Stir the cornstarch slurry into the sauce, mixing until thickened.
19. Serve the chicken with the rice and covered in the sauce.

58 Khichdi Dal

Prep Time: 1 mins; **Cook Time**: 13 mins
Recommended Serving Size: 1 cup; **Serves**: 2

Ingredients:

- ½ c khichdi mix
- 1 c water
- 1 ½ tsp butter
- pinch of salt
- ½ tsp Balti seasoning

Directions:

1. Set the Instant Pot to sauté and add the butter, allowing it to melt.
2. Place in the Balti seasoning and allow it to cook for 1 minute.
3. Mix in the salt, Khichdi, and water, and allow this mixture to come up to a boil.
4. Put on the lid and lock it in place.
5. Set the Instant Pot to rice and cook for 10 minutes.
6. When the time is up, quick release the pressure.
7. Fluff the rice with a fork and serve.

59 Mexican Polenta

Prep Time: 2 mins; **Cook Time**: 20 mins
Recommended Serving Size: 1 cup; **Serves**: 2

Ingredients:

- 1 bunch green onions (scallions)
- 1 tsp garlic, minced
- pinch of cayenne
- 1 ½ tsp chili powder
- ¼ tsp paprika
- 2 tbsp cilantro
- 1 c broth
- ½ tsp oregano
- ½ tsp cumin
- 1 c boiling water
- ½ c corn meal

Directions:

1. Set your Instant Pot to sauté and add in the garlic and onions; allowing them to cook for a few minutes. Keep an eye on it so the garlic doesn't burn, and the onions are softened.
2. Pour in the broth, then add the cilantro, corn meal, spices and boiling water. Stir everything together well.
3. Put on the lid and lock it into place.
4. Set the Instant Pot to high pressure and cook for 5 minutes.
5. When the time is up, allow the pressure to release naturally for 10 minutes, and then quick release the remaining pressure.
6. Stir everything together before serving.

60 Arroz con Pollo

Prep Time: 1 hr; **Cook Time**: 30 mins
Recommended Serving Size: 1 ½ cup; **Serves**: 2

Ingredients:

- 6 boneless chicken thighs

Marinade:

- ¼ tsp pepper
- 1 garlic clove
- 1 ½ tbsp oregano
- 1 tsp cumin
- 2 tbsp olive oil
- 1 tbsp lime juice
- 1 ½ tsp salt

Sofrito:

- 1 garlic clove
- ⅛ tsp pepper
- ¼ yellow onion
- ¼ tsp salt
- ¼ green bell pepper
- handful of cilantro

Rice:

- 1 tbsp coconut oil
- 1 tbsp olive brine
- ½ red bell pepper, chopped
- 14 oz can diced tomatoes

- ⅛ tsp salt
- ½ onion, chopped
- ¾ c Spanish olives, halved
- 1 ½ c long grain brown rice
- ½ tsp cumin
- 3 ½ c stock
- 1 ½ tsp oregano

Directions:

1. Mix all the ingredients together for the marinade and cover the chicken with it. Allow this mixture to chill for at least an hour
2. Pulse the sofrito ingredients together using a food processor or blender.
3. Set your Instant Pot to sauté and add in the oil, allowing it to heat.
4. Place the chicken in and brown on all sides. Take out the chicken and set it aside.
5. Add in the cumin, red bell pepper, onion and oregano to the pot and allow them to cook until the pepper and onion have softened.
6. Mix the sofrito blend into the pot and allow it to cook for 3 minutes.
7. Stir in the tomatoes, salt, stock, and leftover marinade, and allow it all to simmer for 2 minutes.
8. Stir in the olives, rice, and brine.
9. Nestle the chicken into the sauce.
10. Put the lid on and lock it into place.
11. Reset the Instant Pot to meat/stew, and allow it to cook for 15 minutes.
12. When this time is up, use the quick pressure release, serve and enjoy.

61 Rice Pilaf

Prep Time: 10 mins; **Cook Time**: 15 mins
Recommended Serving Size: 1 cup; **Serves**: 2

Ingredients:

- 1 c kale, chopped
- ½ lb green beans, chopped
- ½ lb white mushrooms, halved
- 1 carrot, chopped
- ½ tbsp oyster sauce
- 1 potato, cubed
- 1 tbsp soy sauce
- ½ c leftover meat, chopped
- ½ tbsp vegetable oil
- ½ tbsp rice wine
- 1 ¼ c chicken stock
- 1 c short grain white rice

Directions:

1. Rinse the rice and set in a strainer to drain completely.
2. Mix together the oil, rice, rice wine, and chicken stock in your pot.
3. Add in the kale, green beans, mushrooms, carrot, potato, and meat.
4. Pour the soy sauce over the top, but do not stir everything together.
5. Put on the lid and seal into place.
6. Set the Instant Pot to manual and allow to cook for 8 minutes.

7. When this time is up, allow the pressure to release completely naturally, or you can also use quick release if you would prefer.
8. Carefully stir everything together using a spatula.
9. Mix in the green onions and oyster sauce.
10. Test and adjust any seasonings to taste and serve.

62 Shrimp and Grits

Prep Time: 5 mins; **Cook Time**: 5 hrs
Recommended Serving Size: 1 cup; **Serves**: 2

Ingredients:

- ¾ cup grits
- sriracha sauce
- 1 vegetable bouillion cube
- pinch of salt
- 2 ¼ c water
- 1 ½ tbsp butter
- 1 andouille sausage, chopped
- ¼ cup mozzarella, grated
- 5 oz clean raw shrimp
- ¼ cup cheddar, grated
- 1 clove garlic, minced
- ½ tbsp chili seasoning
- 1/3 cup pepper onion blend

Directions:

1. Add the grits, sausage, bouillon, and water into the bottom of the pot.
2. Put the lid on and seal.
3. Set the Instant Pot to slow cook and cook for 5 hours on low.
4. When the time is up, quick release the pressure then add the remaining ingredients to the pot.
5. Put the lid back on and seal.
6. Keep the Instant Pot on low and cook for an additional 2 hours.

7. When this time is up, quick release the pressure.
8. Serve with a squeeze of sriracha sauce.

63 Farro

Prep Time: 5 mins; **Cook Time**: 15 mins
Recommended Serving Size: 1 cup; **Serves**: 2

Ingredients:

- favorite seasonings
- 1 cup water
- ½ cup farro, rinsed

Directions:

1. Place all the ingredients into the bottom of the pot.
2. Put on the lid and seal.
3. Set the Instant Pot to manual and cook for 10 minutes.
4. When the time is up, naturally release the pressure for 5 minutes, then quick release the remaining pressure.
5. Drain any liquid that remains before serving.

VEGGIES

64 Baked Potatoes

Prep Time: 1 min; **Cook Time**: 10 mins
Recommended Serving Size: 1 potato; **Serves**: 2

Ingredients:

- 2 potatoes

Directions:

1. Set the trivet into the bottom of your pot
2. Place a cup of water into the pot.
3. Set the potatoes on top of the trivet.
4. Put on the lid and lock it into place.
5. Set the Instant Pot to manual and cook for 10 minutes.
6. Allow the pressure to release naturally once the potatoes are done.

65 Maple Bacon Squash

Prep Time: 10 mins; **Cook Time**: 16 mins
Recommended Serving Size: 1 cup; **Serves**: 2

Ingredients:

- 2 lbs acorn squash
- ½ tsp salt
- 1 tbsp butter
- ¼ c cooked bacon, diced
- 1 tbsp maple syrup

Directions:

1. Pour in one cup of water to your pot and set the trivet in.
2. Set the squash on top of the trivet.
3. Put on the lid and seal into place.
4. Set the Instant Pot to manual and cook for 8 mins.
5. When the time is up, allow the pressure to release naturally and let the squash cool.
6. Remove the squash and slice them in half, then remove all the seeds from inside.
7. Place the squash back in.
8. Put the lid back on and seal into place.
9. Keep the Instant Pot to manual and cook
10. When this time is up, quick release the pressure and allow to cool slightly.
11. Remove the squash and scrape the flesh into a bowl, then mash together the butter, maple syrup, and squash. Fold in the bacon and salt before serving.

66 Crispy Potatoes

Prep Time: 5 mins; **Cook Time**: 11 mins
Recommended Serving Size: 4 oz; **Serves**: 2

Ingredients:

- ½ lb fingerling potatoes, peeled
- ½ lemon
- 1 tbsp butter
- ¼ c Italian parsley, minced
- pinch of pepper
- pinch of salt

Directions:

1. Place a half-cup of water in your pot and set in the steamer basket. Set the potatoes on the insert.
2. Put the lid on and lock into place.
3. Set your Instant Pot to high pressure, and cook for 5 minutes.
4. When the time is up, allow the pressure to completely release naturally.
5. Take out the potatoes and pour out all of the water from the pot.
6. Reset the Instant Pot to sauté, add in the butter and let it melt.
7. Place the steamed potatoes back into the pot and sprinkle with the pepper and salt. Allow this to sauté for a few minutes until browned on one side then flip the potatoes over and allow to brown on the other side.
8. Squeeze the lemon juice and sprinkle on the parsley to the potatoes to serve.

67 Mashed Potatoes

Prep Time: 8 mins; **Cook Time**: 10 mins
Recommended Serving Size: 1 cup; **Serves**: 4

Ingredients:

- 2 russet potatoes, quartered and peeled
- pinch of salt
- 1 tbsp butter
- ½ c water
- 1 garlic clove, minced
- pinch of pepper
- ¼ c milk
- 1 tbsp parmesan, grated

Directions:

1. Follow the cooking instructions in the baked potato recipe (64) to cook your potatoes.
2. As the potatoes cook, place the garlic and butter into a separate pan and allow to melt. Mix in the salt and heat until it becomes fragrant.
3. Add in the milk, and deglaze the pan.
4. Once the potatoes are done, take them from the pot and mash in a bowl.
5. Stir in the milk mixture and pepper, parmesan, and salt until well combined

68 Sweet Brussel Sprouts

Prep Time: 3 mins; **Cook Time**: 4 mins
Recommended Serving Size: 4 oz; **Serves**: 2

Ingredients:

- ½ lb brussels sprouts, trimmed
- pinch of salt
- 1 tsp orange zest
- pinch of pepper
- 1 tbsp butter
- 1 ½ tsp maple syrup
- 3 tbsp orange juice

Directions:

1. Place all of the above ingredients into your pot.
2. Put the lid on and lock into place.
3. Set the Instant Pot to manual for 4 minutes. You can cook for less time if you prefer your sprouts to be a bit harder.
4. When the time is up, use the quick pressure release.
5. Mix everything together to make sure that the sprouts are well coated and serve.

69 Bavarian Cabbage

Prep Time: 10 mins; **Cook Time**: 15 mins
Recommended Serving Size: 1 cup; **Serves**: 2

Ingredients:

- 1 cinnamon stick
- 1 ½ tsp brown sugar
- 1 small red cabbage
- 1 tsp salt
- 1 tbsp all-purpose flour
- 1 small onion, diced
- ½ c dry red wine
- ¼ tsp ground cloves
- 1 tbsp butter
- 2 tbsp wine vinegar
- ½ c beef broth
- 1 large apple, peeled, cored and diced
- 1 bay leaf

Directions:

1. Slice the cabbage up, removing the hard core.
2. Set your Instant Pot to sauté and add the butter, allowing it to melt.
3. Add in the onion and apple and cook until they become soft.
4. Turn off the instant pot.
5. Add the cloves, cabbage, brown sugar, wine vinegar, cinnamon, broth, bay leaf, and salt to the pot and mix it together.
6. Add the flour over everything and gently stir it together again.

7. Put the lid on and lock it into place.
8. Reset the Instant Pot to high pressure and cook for 8 minutes.
9. When the time is up, quick release all of the pressure and turn off the pot.
10. Reset the Instant Pot back to sauté and allow the mixture to come to the boil.
11. Mix in the cornstarch and allow the mixture to thicken for 5 minutes.
12. Serve and enjoy.

70 Yogurt Mashed Potatoes

Prep Time: 10 mins; **Cook Time**: 35 mins
Recommended Serving Size: 1 cup; **Serves**: 2

Ingredients:

- pinch of pepper
- ½ c water
- pinch of salt
- ½ tbsp butter
- ½ tsp garlic, minced
- 1 ½ lb baking potatoes, peeled
- ½ c skim milk
- ½ c Greek yogurt

To serve:

cheddar cheese, grated

Directions:

1. Pour the water into your pot and then set the trivet in place.
2. Set the potatoes on top of the trivet.
3. Put on the lid and lock into place.
4. Set your Instant Pot to high pressure and cook for 35 minutes.
5. When the time is up, quick release the pressure and turn off the pot.
6. Carefully remove the trivet, and drain the water out of the pot.
7. Place the potatoes back into the, now dry, pot along with the yogurt, garlic, butter, and quarter cup of milk.
8. Mash the potatoes up with the other ingredients. Mix in more milk if you need to for your desired consistency.

9. Add pepper and salt to your liking.
10. Serve with a sprinkle of cheddar cheese.

71 French Fries

Prep Time: 5 mins; **Cook Time**: 10-20 mins
Recommended Serving Size: ½ the fries; **Serves**: 2

Ingredients:

- 2 large potatoes, sliced into wedges
- frying oil
- 1 tsp coarse salt
- pinch of salt (to serve)
- ¼ tsp baking soda
- 1 c water

Directions:

1. Mix together the baking soda, coarse salt, and water in the pot.
2. Set the trivet in the pot and lay the fries over the top.
3. Put on the lid and lock into place.
4. Set the Instant Pot to high pressure and cook for 2 minutes.
5. Carefully take out the potato wedges, making sure that none of them touches the water. If they do, don't use them unless you dry them off really well.
6. Dab any excess water off the surface of the potato wedges.
7. Empty the water out of the pot, and dry completely.
8. Reset the Instant Pot to sauté and heat up a shallow amount of frying oil, making sure it is really hot before adding any fries.
9. Add some fries to the hot oil and fry to your liking. Make sure that you work in small batches.
10. Remove the fries as they are done and drain on paper towels, sprinkling with salt as they come out.

72 Garlic Potatoes

Prep Time: 5 mins; **Cook Time**: 5 mins
Recommended Serving Size: 1 cup; **Serves**: 2

Ingredients:

- 2 medium russet potatoes
- 3 tbsp parsley
- ½ c broth
- pinch of salt
- 3 garlic cloves, chopped
- ¼ c milk

Directions:

1. Chunk up the potatoes before placing them in the pot. If you want, you can peel the potatoes as well.
2. Add in the broth and garlic.
3. Put the lid on and lock it into place.
4. Set the Instant Pot to high pressure and cook for 4 minutes.
5. When the time is up, allow the pressure to release naturally.
6. Then mash the potatoes up with some added milk to reach the consistency that you like.
7. Add in some parsley and salt to season the potatoes to your liking before serving.

73 Creamed Corn

Prep Time: 5 mins; **Cook Time**: 2 hrs
Recommended Serving Size: 1 cup; **Serves**: 2

Ingredients:

- ½ lb corn kernels
- pinch of pepper
- ½ tsp sugar
- 2 oz cream cheese
- ¼ tsp salt
- 1 tbsp butter
- ¼ c milk

Directions:

1. Mix together the sugar, salt, and corn in the pot, and then pour in the milk.
2. Dot the butter and the cream cheese over the top of the mixture. Make sure you don't mix these in.
3. Put the lid on and lock it into place.
4. Set the Instant Pot to high pressure and cook for 2 hours.
5. When the time is up, quick release the pressure and remove the lid.
6. Stir everything together, making sure the cream cheese and butter are mixed throughout the corn.
7. Add a little extra milk if you want your corn to have a thinner consistency.
8. Season with a little extra pepper and salt if you need to before serving.

74 Corn

Prep Time: 10 mins; **Cook Time**: 2 mins
Recommended Serving Size: 1 corn cob; **Serves**: 2

Ingredients:

- 2 corn cobs
- 2 c water

Directions:

1. Clean the corn cobs well, removing all the silks.
2. Place the water into your pot and place the corn in vertically.
3. Put the lid on and lock it into place.
4. Set the Instant Pot to high pressure and cook for 2 minutes.
5. When the time is up, allow the pressure to release naturally and enjoy.

75 Refried Beans

Prep Time: 5 mins; **Cook Time**: 38 mins
Recommended Serving Size: 1 cup; **Serves**: 2

Ingredients:

- ¼ cup salsa
- ½ tsp salt
- 1 ½ cups water
- 1 cup dried pinto beans, rinsed
- ½ tsp paprika
- 1 medium onion, quartered
- ¼ tsp black pepper
- 1 jalapeno, seeded
- 2 cloves garlic, chopped
- ½ tsp chili powder
- ½ tsp cumin

Directions:

1. Place all the ingredients into the bottom of the pot, stir to combine everything.
2. Put on the lid and seal.
3. Set the Instant Pot to manual and allow to cook for 28 minutes.
4. When the time is up, let sit for 10 minutes before quick releasing the pressure.
5. Carefully open the lid and stir.
6. Use an immersion blender, blend until it is as smooth as you would like. Be careful doing this since the beans are very hot. If there is liquid left on the beans, you may want to drain some of the liquid off before blending so the finished product isn't too thin.

76 Savory Sweet Potato Mash

Prep Time: 5 minutes; **Cook Time**: 9 minutes
Recommended Serving Size: 1 cup; **Serves**: 2

Ingredients:

- ⅛ cup black pepper
- ¼ tsp dried sage
- 1 ½ lbs sweet potatoes, peeled and chopped into cubes
- ½ tsp salt
- ¼ tsp dried rosemary
- ¼ tsp dried parsley
- ⅛ cup milk
- 1 tbsp butter
- ¼ tsp dried thyme
- ¼ cup fresh parmesan, grated
- 1 clove garlic

Directions:

1. Pour one cup or water into the bottom of the pot and place the trivet inside.
2. Place the sweet potatoes and the garlic on the trivet.
3. Put on the lid and seal.
4. Set the Instant Pot on high and cook for 9 minutes.
5. When the time is up, quick release the pressure and drain the water from the pot.
6. Using either a potato masher or electric mixer, mash the garlic and potatoes.
7. Add the remaining ingredients and continue to blend until smooth and creamy.
8. Garnish with parmesan cheese to serve.

DESSERT

77 Banana Polenta Porridge

Prep Time: 1 mins; **Cook Time**: 11 mins
Recommended Serving Size: 1/3 cup; **Serves**: 2

Ingredients:

- 2 tbsp apple juice
- 1 c water
- ⅛ c polenta
- 1/3 c rice
- 1 ½ tbsp lemon juice
- ½ tsp vanilla essence
- 1 c milk
- 1 banana, chopped
- pinch of turmeric

Directions:

1. Put all of the above ingredients, minus the polenta, into your pot and mix together.
2. Set the Instant Pot to sauté and allow the mix to come to the boil.
3. Turn the sauté setting off.
4. Put on the lid and lock into place.
5. Reset the Instant Pot to high pressure and cook for 5 minutes.

6. When the time is up, quick release the pressure and take off the lid.
7. Whisk the polenta into the mixture.
8. Once it has thickened, serve and enjoy.

78 Christmas Pudding

Prep Time: 20 mins; **Cook Time**: 50 mins
Recommended Serving Size: ½ pudding; **Serves**: 2

Ingredients:

- 2/3 c dried cranberries, let them soak for 30 minutes
- 1 medium carrot, grated
- ⅛ tsp olive oil
- 1 c sugar
- 2/3 c dried apricots, chopped
- pinch of salt
- ½ tsp cinnamon
- 3 tbsp maple syrup
- 3 tsp baking powder
- 4 eggs
- 15 tbsp butter, chopped
- 1 c all-purpose flour
- 1 tsp ginger

Directions:

1. Cover all of the dried fruit with boiling water.
2. Take a heatproof bowl and coat it with olive oil. Make sure to coat the whole of the insides.
3. If the bowl doesn't have handles, make a sling with some aluminum foil.
4. Pour in two cups of water to the bottom of the pot and set in the steamer basket.

5. Place the salt, flour, ginger, sugar, baking powder, and cinnamon in a food processor. Pulse everything together until it is all mixed.
6. Then add the butter to the processor and pulse it all together.
7. Pour this batter into a bowl and mix in the eggs and syrup.
8. Strain the water off the fruit and stir the carrot into this.
9. Mix the fruit and carrot into the batter using a knife.
10. Pour the mixture into your oiled bowl and slowly place it into the pot, setting it on top of the basket.
11. Put the lid on the pot, but don't use any pressure
12. Set the Instant Pot to sauté, and once you see steam starting to be released, time the pudding for 15 minutes.
13. When the time is up, seal the lid in place.
14. Reset the Instant Pot to high pressure and cook for a further 35 minutes.
15. When this time is up, quick release the pressure.
16. Carefully remove the pudding, and turn it out onto a plate to serve.

79 Red Wine Pears

Prep Time: 2 mins; **Cook Time**: 12 mins
Recommended Serving Size: 1 pear; **Serves**: 2

Ingredients:

- 2 pears, peeled
- ½ c sugar
- ¼ bottle of your favorite red wine
- 1 piece of ginger
- 1 clove
- 1 cinnamon stick

Directions:

1. Place the wine into your pot.
2. Mix in the ginger, cinnamon, sugar, and clove.
3. Set the pears into the mixture.
4. Put the lid in place and lock.
5. Set the Instant Pot to high and cook for 6 minutes.
6. When the time is up, quick release the pressure.
7. Remove the lid and carefully take out the pears, setting them aside.
8. Switch the pot to sauté and let the liquid cook until it reduces by half.
9. Drizzle the juice over the pears to serve.

80 Baked Apples

Prep Time: 5 mins; **Cook Time**: 20 mins
Recommended Serving Size: 1 apple; **Serves**: 2

Ingredients:

- 2 apples, cored
- ½ tsp cinnamon
- 3 tbsp raisins
- ¼ c sugar
- ¼ c red wine

Directions:

1. Set the apples into the bottom of the pot.
2. Place in the wine, cinnamon, raisins, and sugar.
3. Put the lid on and seal it into place.
4. Set the Instant Pot to high pressure and cook for 10 minutes.
5. When this time is up, allow the pressure to release naturally for 10 minutes, and then quickly release the rest of the pressure.
6. Carefully take the apples out and put in bowls to serve with the juice poured over.

81 Key Lime Pie

Prep Time: 15 mins; **Cook Time**: 25 mins and 4 hrs chill time
Recommended Serving Size: 1/6 pie; **Serves**: 6

Ingredients:

Crust:

- 3 tbsp butter, melted
- 1 tbsp sugar
- ¾ c graham-cracker crumbs

Filling:

- 1 can sweetened condensed milk
- 2 tbsp key lime zest
- 1/3 c sour cream
- 4 large egg yolks
- ½ c key lime juice

Directions:

1. Take a seven inch springform pan and coat it with cooking oil
2. Combine the graham cracker crumbs, sugar, and butter together. Place this crust into the springform pan and put in the freezer to chill for 10 minutes.
3. Beat the yolks together until they become light.
4. Mix in the milk until it starts to thicken, and then add in the juice.
5. Fold the sour cream and zest into the filling mixture.
6. Take the crust out of the freezer and place the filling mixture into the pan.
7. Cover the cheesecake with aluminum foil.
8. Pour 1 cup of water into the pot, and then set in the trivet.

9. Make a foil sling and place it under the pan, easing this into the pot.
10. Put on the lid and lock into place.
11. Set the Instant Pot to high pressure and cook for 15 minutes.
12. When the time is up, allow the pressure to release naturally for 10 minutes, and then quickly release the rest of the pressure.
13. Carefully remove the pan and place on a cooling rack to cool.
14. Place the cooled pan into the fridge for 4 hours.
15. Serve chilled with whipped cream.

82 Chocolate Cake

Prep Time: 15 mins; **Cook Time**: 50 mins
Recommended Serving Size: 1/6 of the cake; **Serves**: 6

Ingredients:

- ¾ c all-purpose flour
- ¾ tsp baking soda
- 3 tbsp cocoa powder
- ¼ c milk
- ½ tsp vanilla essence
- 3 tbsp butter, softened
- ¼ c water
- ¼ tsp salt
- ½ tsp lemon juice
- 1 egg
- ½ c sugar

Directions:

1. Mix together the baking soda, salt, and flour.
2. In a larger bowl, combine the butter and sugar until they become creamy.
3. Beat the egg until it becomes fluffy.
4. Whisk the water and the cocoa into the sugar mixture until they are well incorporated.
5. Stir in the vanilla, lemon juice, and the milk.
6. Slowly and carefully fold the flour mixture into the sugar mixture, making sure that you don't overmix the batter.
7. Take a six-inch cake pan and grease well with butter.
8. Pour the prepared batter into the greased cake pan.

9. Place a tray or plate on the bottom of the pot.

10. Set the Instant Pot to warm and allow it to heat, you don't need water or gasket.

11. After the pot has heated up for two minutes, gently set the cake pan into the cooker. Use an aluminum foil sling to help to place the cake in and take it out when cooked.

12. Put the lid and on and seal

13. Reset the Instant Pot to low and allow the cake to cook for about 45 to 50 minutes. You should notice the cake pulling off the pan's sides, and a toothpick to test should come out clean.

14. Once it is cooked, let the cake cool for ten minutes, and then flip the cake out onto a plate.

15. You can enjoy the cake as it is, or you can frost it with your favorite flavor of frosting.

83 Oreo Cheesecake

Prep Time: 30 mins; **Cook Time**: 8 hrs 40 mins
Recommended Serving Size: 1/6 cake; **Serves**: 6

Ingredients:

Crust:
- 12 crushed Oreos
- 2 tbsp melted butter

Cake:
- ½ c sugar
- 16 oz cream cheese
- 2 eggs
- 8 Oreos, chopped
- 1 tbsp all-purpose flour
- ¼ c heavy cream
- 2 tsp vanilla essence

Topping:
- 1 c whipped cream
- 8 Oreos, chopped

Directions:

1. Place aluminum foil over the bottom of a seven inch springform pan and spray with cooking spray.
2. Combine together the crushed cookies and melted butter, and press them into your prepared pan.
3. Place this in your freezer and freeze for 15 minutes.
4. With a stand mixer, beat the cream cheese until it becomes a smooth consistency.

5. Then beat in the sugar and then the eggs until they are all well mixed.
6. Make sure you scrape the sides of the bowl down from time to time
7. Next, beat in the cream, vanilla essence, and flour until it is smooth.
8. Once well mixed, carefully fold in the eight chopped Oreos, and then pour this mixture into the prepared pan.
9. Cover the cheesecake with aluminum foil.
10. Pour a cup and a half of water into the pot and then set in the trivet.
11. Make a foil sling and place it under the pan, then carefully ease the pan onto the trivet.
12. Put on the lid and lock it in place.
13. Set the Instant Pot to high pressure, and let it cook for 40 minutes.
14. When the time is up, turn off the pot and let the pressure release naturally for 10 minutes and then quick release the rest of the pressure.
15. Carefully remove the pan using the foil sling and place it on a cooling rack.
16. Once at room temperature, place the pan in the fridge and leave it to chill for at least 8 hours before cutting.
17. Serve the cake topped with chopped cookies and whipped cream.

84 Peanut Butter Chocolate Cheesecake

Prep Time: 10 mins; **Cook Time**: 2 hrs 6 mins
Recommended Serving Size: 1 jar; **Serves**: 2

Ingredients:

- 4 oz cream cheese
- 1 egg
- ¼ tsp vanilla essence
- 2 tbsp sugar
- 1 ½ tsp powdered peanut butter
- ¾ tsp cocoa powder

Directions:

1. All of your ingredients should be at room temperature.
2. Cream together the cream cheese and the eggs until they are completely smooth.
3. Stir in all the other ingredients.
4. Take two eight-ounce mason jars and divide the batter between the two jars, then cover the tops of the jars with foil.
5. Place one cup of water and the trivet into your pot.
6. Place the jars on the trivet carefully.
7. Put on the lid and lock into place.
8. Set the Instant Pot to high pressure and cook for 16 minutes.
9. When the time is up, allow the pressure to release naturally.
10. Carefully remove the jars and let them chill in the fridge for a couple of hours.
11. Serve the cheesecake jars topped with whipped cream.

85 *Cranberry Bread Pudding*

Prep Time: 15 mins; **Cook Time**: 25 mins
Recommended Serving Size: 1 cup; **Serves**: 2

Ingredients:

- 2 eggs
- 1 c milk
- whipped cream
- ¼ c sugar
- ¾ c water
- 3 tbsp nuts, chopped
- ½ tsp vanilla essence
- 1 ½ c bread cubes, dried
- 3 tbsp dried cranberries

Directions:

1. Grease a small soufflé dish well and make an aluminum foil sling to help place the dish into the pot.
2. Beat together the eggs, vanilla, milk, and sugar.
3. Place the bread and the cranberries into your prepared soufflé dish.
4. Place the custard mixture on top of this bread mix, and cover the dish with aluminum foil.
5. Pour a cup and half of water into the pot and set in the trivet.
6. Lower the dish into the pot using the sling you made earlier.
7. Put on the lid and lock it into place.
8. Set the Instant Pot to high pressure and cook for 25 minutes.
9. When the time is up, quick release the pressure.
10. Carefully lift the dish out of the pot.
11. Serve warm with a topping of whipped cream.

86 Salted Caramel Cheesecake

Prep Time: 20 mins; **Cook Time**: 4 hours 35 minutes
Recommended Serving Size: 1/6 cake; **Serves**: 6

Ingredients:

Crust:

- 4 tbsp butter, melted
- 2 tbsp sugar
- 1 ½ c Ritz crackers, crushed

Cake:

- 16 oz cream cheese
- 1 ½ tsp vanilla essence
- 2 eggs
- ½ tsp kosher salt
- ½ c brown sugar
- 1 tbsp flour
- ¼ c sour cream

Top:

- ½ c caramel sauce
- 1 tsp sea salt

Directions:

1. Take a seven inch springform pan and spray it with cooking spray. Place parchment paper along the bottom of the pan and then spray with some more cooking spray.
2. Stir together the ritz crackers, butter, and sugar and use this to make the crust in your prepared springform pan

3. With a stand mixer, beat the sugar and the cream cheese together until they are smooth.
4. Mix in the sour cream, and then the flour, salt, and vanilla. Scraping the sides down when you need to.
5. Beat in the eggs.
6. Pour the cake mixture into the prepared pan.
7. Pour two cups of water into your pot and then set in the trivet.
8. Wrap the bottom of it with foil, and the wrap a foil sling around the pan to help with removing the pan.
9. Set the pan onto the trivet.
10. Put the lid on and seal it.
11. Set the Instant Pot to high pressure and cook for 35 minutes.
12. When the time is up, allow the pressure to release naturally.
13. Carefully remove the pan from the pot and set on a wire rack to cool.
14. Once it reaches room temperature, place it in the fridge to chill for 4 hours.
15. When it is set and cooled completely, top with some sea salt and caramel sauce.

87 Pineapple Upside Down Cake

Prep Time: 20 mins; **Cook Time**: 1 hr
Recommended Serving Size: 1/6 cake; **Serves**: 6

Ingredients:

- 1 tsp butter
- 2 eggs
- 2 tbsp sugar
- 6 slices pineapple
- ¼ c milk
- 3 tbsp pineapple juice
- 1 ½ c all-purpose flour
- ½ tsp baking soda
- 1 c powdered sugar
- ½ c butter
- maraschino cherries
- 1 tsp baking powder

Directions:

1. Grease a cake pan that will fit in your instant pot and then sprinkle it with two tablespoons of sugar.
2. Place the pineapple slices across the pan bottom and set a cherry in the center of each of the pineapple slices.
3. In a bowl beat the eggs together until fluffy, and then add in the salt and sugar.
4. Stir in the juice, oil, and milk.
5. In a separate bowl mix the baking soda, flour, and baking powder together.

6. Slowly fold the flour mixture into the egg mixture.
7. Once well incorporated, pour the batter into the prepared pan.
8. Set a rack inside your pot and allow it to heat on warm for 10 minutes.
9. Place a foil sling around the cake pan and ease it into the pot.
10. Put on the lid and lock into place.
11. Set the Instant Pot to medium and allow it to cook for 40 minutes.
12. Use a toothpick to check for the sponge is cooked through.
13. Carefully take the cake out and allow it to cool for 30 minutes.
14. Once cool, flip the cake out onto a plate before serving.

CONCLUSION

Thanks again for buying and reading, *Instant Pot Cookbook for Two: Quick, Easy and Delicious Instant Pot Recipes for Two*. This book contains over 85 quick and easy recipes, all crafted for at least 2 servings, which you can use for breakfast, lunch, and dinner.

The next step is to grab your Instant Pot and start trying some of these delicious recipes for two. Hopefully, by trying out some of these recipes using the Instant Pot machine, everyday cooking will be a bit more colorful, and pack a lot of flavorful punches.

Finally, if you found this book useful in any way, a review on Amazon is always appreciated!

CPSIA information can be obtained
at www.ICGtesting.com
Printed in the USA
FSHW04n1935130318
45692FS